AWS Organizations User Guide

A catalogue record for this book is available from the Hong Kong Public Libraries.

Published in Hong Kong by Samurai Media Limited.

Email: info@samuraimedia.org

ISBN 9789888407750

Contents

What Is AWS Organizations?

AWS Organizations is an account management service that enables you to consolidate multiple AWS accounts into an *organization* that you create and centrally manage. AWS Organizations includes consolidated billing and account management capabilities that enable you to better meet the budgetary, security, and compliance needs of your business. As an administrator of an organization, you can create accounts in your organization and invite existing accounts to join the organization.

This user guide defines key concepts for AWS Organizations and explains how to use the service.

AWS Organizations Features

AWS Organizations offers the following features:

Centralized management of all of your AWS accounts
You can combine your existing accounts into an organization that enables you to manage the accounts centrally. You can create accounts that automatically are a part of your organization, and you can invite other accounts to join your organization. You also can attach policies that affect some or all of your accounts.

Consolidated billing for all member accounts
Consolidated billing is a feature of AWS Organizations. You can use the master account of your organization to consolidate and pay for all member accounts.

Hierarchical grouping of your accounts to meet your budgetary, security, or compliance needs
You can group your accounts into organizational units (OUs) and attach different access policies to each OU. For example, if you have accounts that must access only the AWS services that meet certain regulatory requirements, you can put those accounts into one OU. You then can attach a policy to that OU that blocks access to services that do not meet those regulatory requirements. You can nest OUs within other OUs to a depth of five levels, providing flexibility in how you structure your account groups.

Control over the AWS services and API actions that each account can access
As an administrator of the master account of an organization, you can restrict which AWS services and individual API actions the users and roles in each member account can access. This restriction even overrides the administrators of member accounts in the organization. When AWS Organizations blocks access to a service or API action for a member account, a user or role in that account can't access any prohibited service or API action, even if an administrator of a member account explicitly grants such permissions in an IAM policy. Organization permissions overrule account permissions.

Integration and support for AWS Identity and Access Management (IAM)
IAM provides granular control over users and roles in individual accounts. AWS Organizations expands that control to the account level by giving you control over what users and roles in an account or a group of accounts can do. The resulting permissions are the logical intersection of what is allowed by AWS Organizations at the account level, and what permissions are explicitly granted by IAM at the user or role level within that account. In other words, the user can access only what is allowed by **both** the AWS Organizations policies and IAM policies. If either blocks an operation, the user can't access that operation.

Integration with other AWS services
You can enable select AWS services to access accounts in your organization and perform actions on the resources in the accounts. When you configure another service and authorize it to access with your organization, AWS Organizations creates an IAM service-linked role for that service in each member account. The service-linked role has predefined IAM permissions that allow the other AWS service to perform specific tasks in your organization and its accounts. For this to work, all accounts in an organization automatically have a service-linked role that enables the AWS Organizations service to create the service-linked roles required by AWS services for which you enable trusted access. These additional service-linked roles come with policies that enable the specified service to perform only those tasks that are required by your configuration choices. For more information, see Enabling Trusted Access with Other AWS Services.

Data replication that is eventually consistent

AWS Organizations, like many other AWS services, is eventually consistent. AWS Organizations achieves high availability by replicating data across multiple servers in AWS data centers within its region. If a request to change some data is successful, the change is committed and safely stored. However, the change must then be replicated across the multiple servers. For more information, see Changes that I make aren't always immediately visible.

AWS Organizations Pricing

AWS Organizations is offered at no additional charge. You are charged only for AWS resources that users and roles in your member accounts use. For example, you are charged the standard fees for Amazon EC2 instances that are used by users or roles in your member accounts. For information about the pricing of other AWS services, see AWS Pricing.

Accessing AWS Organizations

You can work with AWS Organizations in any of the following ways:

AWS Management Console

The AWS Organizations console is a browser-based interface that you can use to manage your organization and your AWS resources. You can perform any task in your organization by using the console.

AWS Command Line Tools

The AWS command line tools allow you to issue commands at your system's command line to perform AWS Organizations and AWS tasks; this can be faster and more convenient than using the console. The command line tools also are useful if you want to build scripts that perform AWS tasks.

AWS provides two sets of command line tools: the AWS Command Line Interface (AWS CLI) and the AWS Tools for Windows PowerShell. For information about installing and using the AWS CLI, see the AWS Command Line Interface User Guide. For information about installing and using the Tools for Windows PowerShell, see the AWS Tools for Windows PowerShell User Guide.

AWS SDKs

The AWS SDKs consist of libraries and sample code for various programming languages and platforms (for example, Java, Python, Ruby, .NET, iOS, and Android). The SDKs take care of tasks such as cryptographically signing requests, managing errors, and retrying requests automatically. For more information about the AWS SDKs, including how to download and install them, see Tools for Amazon Web Services.

AWS Organizations HTTPS Query API

The AWS Organizations HTTPS Query API gives you programmatic access to AWS Organizations and AWS. The HTTPS Query API lets you issue HTTPS requests directly to the service. When you use the HTTPS API, you must include code to digitally sign requests using your credentials. For more information, see Calling the API by Making HTTP Query Requests and the AWS Organizations API Reference.

Support and Feedback for AWS Organizations

We welcome your feedback. You can send comments to feedback-awsorganizations@amazon.com. You also can post your feedback and questions in AWS Organizations support forum. For more information about the AWS support forums, see Forums Help.

Other AWS Resources

- **AWS Training and Courses** – Links to role-based and specialty courses as well as self-paced labs to help sharpen your AWS skills and gain practical experience.

- **AWS Developer Tools** – Links to developer tools and resources that provide documentation, code examples, release notes, and other information to help you build innovative applications with AWS.
- **AWS Support Center** – The hub for creating and managing your AWS Support cases. Also includes links to other helpful resources, such as forums, technical FAQs, service health status, and AWS Trusted Advisor.
- **AWS Support** – The primary webpage for information about AWS Support, a one-on-one, fast-response support channel to help you build and run applications in the cloud.
- **Contact Us** – A central contact point for inquiries concerning AWS billing, account, events, abuse, and other issues.
- **AWS Site Terms** – Detailed information about our copyright and trademark; your account, license, and site access; and other topics.

Getting Started with AWS Organizations

The following topics provide information to help you start learning and using AWS Organizations.

Learn about ...

AWS Organizations Terminology and Concepts
Learn the terminology and core concepts needed to understand AWS Organizations. This section describes each of the components of an organization and the basics of how they work together to provide a new level of control over what users in those accounts can do.

Consolidated Billing for Organizations One of the primary features about AWS Organizations is the consolidation of the billing of all of the accounts in your organization. Learn more about how billing is handled in an organization and how various discounts work when shared across multiple accounts. This content is in the *AWS Billing and Cost Management User Guide*.

AWS Organizations Terminology and Concepts

To help you get started with AWS Organizations, this topic explains some of the key concepts.

The following diagram shows a basic organization that consists of seven accounts that are organized into four organizational units (OUs) under the root. The organization also has several policies that are attached to some of the OUs or directly to accounts. For a description of each of these items, refer to the definitions in this topic.

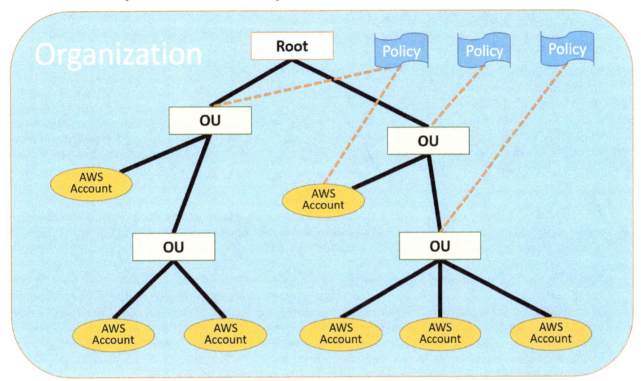

Organization An entity that you create to consolidate your AWS accounts. You can use the AWS Organizations console to centrally view and manage all of your accounts within your organization. An organization has one master account along with zero or more member accounts. You can organize the accounts in a hierarchical, tree-like structure with a root at the top and organizational units nested under the root. Each account can be directly in the root, or placed in one of the OUs in the hierarchy. An organization has the functionality that is determined by the feature set that you enable.

Root The parent container for all the accounts for your organization. If you apply a policy to the root, it applies to all organizational units (OUs) and accounts in the organization.
Currently, you can have only one root. AWS Organizations automatically creates it for you when you create an organization.

Organization unit (OU) A container for accounts within a root. An OU also can contain other OUs, enabling you to create a hierarchy that resembles an upside-down tree, with a root at the top and branches of OUs that reach down, ending in accounts that are the leaves of the tree. When you attach a policy to one of the nodes in the hierarchy, it flows down and affects all the branches (OUs) and leaves (accounts) beneath it. An OU can have exactly one parent, and currently each account can be a member of exactly one OU.

Account A standard AWS account that contains your AWS resources. You can attach a policy to an account to apply controls to only that one account.
An organization has one account that is designated as the *master account*. This is the account that creates the organization. The rest of the accounts that belong to an organization are called *member accounts*. From the organization's master account, you can create accounts in the organization, invite other existing accounts to the organization, remove accounts from the organization, manage invitations, and apply policies to entities (roots, OUs, or accounts) within the organization. An account can be a member of only one organization at a time.

The master account has the responsibilities of a *payer account* and is responsible for paying all charges that are accrued by the member accounts.

Invitation The process of asking another account to join your organization. An invitation can be issued only by the organization's master account and is extended to either the account ID or the email address that is associated with the invited account. After the invited account accepts an invitation, it becomes a member account in the organization. Invitations also can be sent to all current member accounts when the organization needs all members to approve the change from supporting only consolidated billing features to supporting all features in the organization. Invitations work by accounts exchanging handshakes. Although you might not see handshakes when you work in the AWS Organizations console, if you use the AWS CLI or AWS Organizations API, you must work directly with handshakes.

Handshake A multi-step process of exchanging information between two parties. One of its primary uses in AWS Organizations is to serve as the underlying implementation for invitations. Handshake messages are passed between and responded to by the handshake initiator and the recipient in such a way that it ensures that both parties always know what the current status is. Handshakes also are used when changing the organization from supporting only consolidated billing features to supporting all features that AWS Organizations offers. You generally need to directly interact with handshakes only if you work with the AWS Organizations API or command line tools such as the AWS CLI.

Available feature sets

- **Consolidated billing** – This feature set provides shared billing functionality, but does *not* include the more advanced features of AWS Organizations, such as the use of policies to restrict what users and roles in different accounts can do. To use the advanced AWS Organizations features, you must enable all features in your organization.
- **All features** – The complete feature set that is available to AWS Organizations. It includes all the functionality of consolidated billing, plus advanced features that give you more control over accounts in your organization. For example, when all features are enabled the master account of the organization has full control over what member accounts can do. The master account can apply SCPs to restrict the services and actions that users (including the root user) and roles in an account can access, and it can prevent member accounts from leaving the organization. You can create an organization with all features already enabled, or you can enable all features in an organization that originally supported only the consolidated billing features. To enable all features, all invited member accounts must approve the change by accepting the invitation that is sent when the master account starts the process.

Service control policy (SCP) A policy that specifies the services and actions that users and roles can use in the accounts that the SCP affects. SCPs are similar to IAM permission policies except that they don't grant any permissions. Instead, SCPs are *filters* that allow only the specified services and actions to be used in affected accounts. Even if a user is granted full administrator permissions with an IAM permission policy, any access that is not explicitly allowed or that is explicitly denied by the SCPs affecting that account is blocked. For example, if you assign an SCP that allows only database service access to your "database" account, then any user, group, or role in that account is denied access to any other service's operations. SCPs are available only when you enable all features in your organization. You can attach an SCP to the following:

- A root, which affects all accounts in the organization
- An OU, which affects all accounts in that OU and all accounts in any OUs in that OU subtree
- An individual account The master account of the organization is not affected by any SCPs that are attached either to it or to any root or OU the master account might be in.

Whitelisting vs. blacklisting Whitelisting and blacklisting are complementary techniques that you can use when you apply SCPs to filter the permissions that are available to accounts.

- **Whitelisting** – You explicitly specify the access that *is* allowed. All other access is implicitly blocked. By default, AWS Organizations attaches an AWS managed policy called `FullAWSAccess` to all roots, OUs, and accounts. This ensures that, as you build your organization, nothing is blocked until you want it to be. In other words, by default all permissions are whitelisted. When you are ready to restrict permissions, you *replace* the `FullAWSAccess` policy with one that allows only the more limited, desired set of permissions.

Users and roles in the affected accounts can then exercise only that level of access, even if their IAM policies allow all actions. If you replace the default policy on the root, all accounts in the organization are affected by the restrictions. You can't add them back at a lower level in the hierarchy because an SCP never grants permissions; it only filters them.

- **Blacklisting** – You explicitly specify the access that *is **not*** allowed. All other access is allowed. In this scenario, all permissions are allowed unless explicitly blocked. This is the default behavior of AWS Organizations. By default, AWS Organizations attaches an AWS managed policy called `FullAWSAccess` to all roots, OUs, and accounts. This allows any account to access any service or operation with no AWS Organizations–imposed restrictions. Unlike the whitelisting technique described above, when using blacklists you typically leave the default `FullAWSAccess` policy in place (that allow "all") but then attach additional policies that explicitly ***deny*** access to the unwanted services and actions. Just as with IAM permission policies, an explicit deny of a service action overrides any allow of that action.

AWS Organizations Tutorials

Use the tutorials in this section to learn how to perform tasks using AWS Organizations.

Tutorial: Creating and Configuring an Organization
Get up and running with step-by-step instructions to create your organization, invite your first member accounts, create an OU hierarchy that contains your accounts, and apply some service control policies (SCPs).

Tutorial: Monitor Important Changes to Your Organization with CloudWatch Events
Monitor key changes in your organization by configuring Amazon CloudWatch Events to trigger an alarm in the form of an email, SMS text message, or log entry when actions that you designate occur in your organization. For example, many organizations want to know when a new account is created or when an account attempts to leave the organization.

Tutorial: Creating and Configuring an Organization

In this tutorial, you create your organization and configure it with two AWS member accounts. You create one of the member accounts in your organization, and you invite the other account to join your organization. Next, you use the whitelisting technique to specify that account administrators can delegate only explicitly listed services and actions. This allows administrators to validate any new service that AWS introduces before they permit its use by anyone else in your company. That way, if AWS introduces a new service, it remains prohibited until an administrator adds the service to the whitelist in the appropriate policy. The tutorial also shows you how to use blacklisting to ensure that no users in a member account can change the configuration for the auditing logs that are created by AWS CloudTrail.

The following illustration shows the main steps of the tutorial.

Step 1: Create Your Organization
In this step, you create an organization with your current AWS account as the master account. You also invite one AWS account to join your organization, and you create a second account as a member account.

Step 2: Create the Organizational Units
Next, you create two organizational units (OUs) in your new organization and place the member accounts in those OUs.

Step 3: Create the Service Control Policies
You can apply restrictions to what actions can be delegated to users and roles in the member accounts by using service control policies (SCPs). An SCP is a type of organization control policy. In this step, you create two SCPs and attach them to the OUs in your organization.

Step 4: Testing Your Organization's Policies
You can sign in as users from each of the test accounts and see the effects that the SCPs have on the accounts.

None of the steps in this tutorial incur costs to your AWS bill. AWS Organizations is a free service.

Prerequisites

This tutorial assumes that you have access to two existing AWS accounts (you create a third as part of this tutorial) and that you can sign in to each as an administrator.

The tutorial refers to the accounts as the following:

- 111111111111 – The account that you use to create the organization. This account becomes the master account. The owner of this account has an email address of masteraccount@example.com.
- 222222222222 – An account that you invite to join the organization as a member account. The owner of this account has an email address of member222@example.com.
- 333333333333 – An account that you create as a member of the organization. The owner of this account has an email address of member333@example.com.

Substitute the values above with the values that are associated with your test accounts. We recommend that you do not use production accounts for this tutorial.

Step 1: Create Your Organization

In this step, you sign in to account 111111111111 as an administrator, create an organization with that account as the master, and invite an existing account, 222222222222, to join as a member account.

1. Sign in to AWS as an administrator of account 111111111111 and open the AWS Organizations console at https://console.aws.amazon.com/organizations/.

2. On the introduction page, choose **Create organization**.

3. In the **Create new organization** dialog box, choose **ENABLE ALL FEATURES** and then choose **Create organization**.

4. Choose **Settings** in the upper-right corner and confirm that your organization has all features enabled by looking at the box in the lower-left corner of the page.

You now have an organization with your account as its only member. This is the master account of the organization.

Invite an Existing Account to Join Your Organization

Now that you have an organization, you can begin to populate it with accounts. In the steps in this section, you invite an existing account to join as a member of your organization.

To invite an existing account to join

1. Open the Organizations console at https://console.aws.amazon.com/organizations/.

2. Choose the **Accounts** tab. The star next to the account name indicates that it is the master account.

   Now you can invite other accounts to join as member accounts.

3. On the **Accounts** tab, choose **Add account** and then choose **Invite account**.

4. In the **Account ID or email** box, type the email address of the owner of the account that you want to invite, similar to the following: **account222@example.com**

5. Type any text that you want into the **Notes** box. This text is included in the email that is sent to the owner of the account.

6. Choose **Invite**. AWS Organizations sends the invitation to the account owner. **Important**
   If you get an error that indicates that you exceeded your account limits for the organization or that you can't add an account because your organization is still initializing, wait until one hour after you created the organization and try again. If the error persists, contact AWS Support.

7. For the purposes of this tutorial, you now need to accept your own invitation. Do one of the following to get to the **Invitations** page in the console:

   - Open the email that AWS sent from the master account and choose the link to accept the invitation. When prompted to sign in, do so as an administrator in the invited member account.
   - Open the AWS Organizations console (https://console.aws.amazon.com/organizations/) and sign in as an administrator of the member account. Choose **Invitations**. The number beside the link indicates how many invitations this account has.

8. On the **Invitations** page, choose **Accept** and then choose **Confirm**.

9. Sign out of your member account and sign in again as an administrator in your master account.

Create a Member Account

In the steps in this section, you create an AWS account that is automatically a member of the organization. We refer to this account in the tutorial as 333333333333.

To create a member account

1. On the AWS Organizations console, on the **Accounts** tab, choose **Add account**.

2. For **Full name**, type a name for the account, such as **MainApp Account**.

3. For **Email**, type the email address of the individual who is to receive communications on behalf of the account. This value must be globally unique. No two accounts can have the same email address. For example, you might use something like **mainapp@example.com**.

4. For **IAM role name**, you can leave this blank to automatically use the default role name of `OrganizationAccountAccessRole`, or you can supply your own name. This role enables you to access the new member account when signed in as an IAM user in the master account. For this tutorial, leave it blank to instruct AWS Organizations to create the role with the default name.

5. Choose **Create**. You might need to wait a short while and refresh the page to see the new account appear on the **Accounts** tab. **Important**
If you get an error that indicates that you exceeded your account limits for the organization or that you can't add an account because your organization is still initializing, wait until one hour after you created the organization and try again. If the error persists, contact AWS Support.

Step 2: Create the Organizational Units

In the steps in this section, you create organizational units (OUs) and place your member accounts in them. Your hierarchy looks like the following illustration when you are done. The master account remains in the root. One member account is moved to the Production OU, and the other member account is moved to the MainApp OU, which is a child of Production.

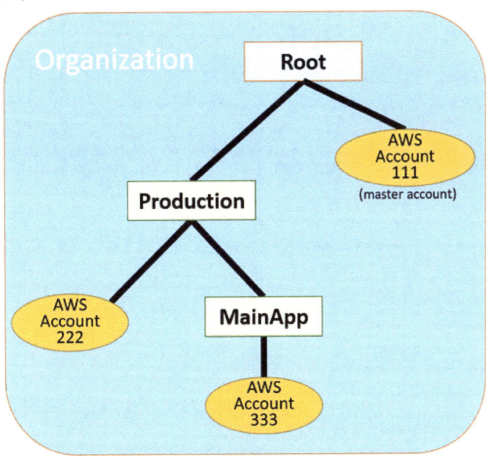

To create and populate the OUs

1. On the AWS Organizations console, choose the **Organize Accounts** tab and then choose **+ New organizational unit**.

2. For the name of the OU, type **Production** and then choose **Create organizational unit**.

3. Choose your new **Production** OU to navigate into it, and then choose **+ New organizational unit**.

4. For the name of the second OU, type **MainApp** and then choose **Create organizational unit**.

17

Now you can move your member accounts into these OUs.

5. In the tree view on the left, choose the **Root**.

6. Select the first member account 222222222222, and then choose **Move**.

7. In the **Move accounts** dialog box, choose **Production** and then choose **Move**.

8. Select the second member account 333333333333, and then choose **Move**.

9. In the **Move accounts** dialog box, choose **Production** to expose **MainApp**. Choose **MainApp**, and then choose **Move**.

Step 3: Create the Service Control Policies

In the steps in this section, you create three service control policies (SCPs) and attach them to the root and to the OUs to restrict what users in the organization's accounts can do. The first SCP prevents anyone in any of the member accounts from creating or modifying any AWS CloudTrail logs that you configure. The master account is not affected by any SCP, so after you apply the CloudTrail SCP you must create any logs from the master account.

To create the first SCP that blocks CloudTrail configuration actions

1. Choose the **Policies** tab, and then choose **Create policy**.

2. Choose **Policy generator**.

3. For **Policy name**, type **Block CloudTrail Configuration Actions**.

4. For **Choose Overall Effect**, choose **Deny**.

5. In the **Statement builder**, for **Select service** select **AWS CloudTrail**. For **Select action**, choose the following actions: **AddTags**, **CreateTrail**, **DeleteTrail**, **RemoveTags**, **StartLogging**, **StopLogging**, and **UpdateTrail**.

6. Choose **Add statement** to add it to the list of statements for the SCP, and then choose **Create policy** to save it to your organization.

7. Choose the new policy in the list, and then choose **Policy editor** to view the new policy's JSON content. It looks similar to the following:

```
1  {
2      "Version": "2012-10-17",
3      "Statement": [
4          {
5              "Sid": "Stmt1234567890123",
6              "Effect": "Deny",
7              "Action": [
8                  "cloudtrail:AddTags",
9                  "cloudtrail:CreateTrail",
10                 "cloudtrail:DeleteTrail",
11                 "cloudtrail:RemoveTags",
12                 "cloudtrail:StartLogging",
13                 "cloudtrail:StopLogging",
14                 "cloudtrail:UpdateTrail"
15             ],
16             "Resource": [
17                 "*"
18             ]
19         }
20     ]
```

```
21 }
```

The second policy defines a whitelist of all the services and actions that you want to enable for users and roles in the Production OU. When you are done, users in the Production OU can access **only** the listed services and actions.

To create the second policy that whitelists approved services for the Production OU

1. Choose **All policies** at the top of the page to go back to the list, choose **Create policy**, and then choose **Policy generator**.

2. For **Policy name**, type **Whitelist for All Approved Services**.

3. For **Choose Overall Effect**, choose **Allow**.

4. In the **Statement builder**, select **Amazon EC2**. For **Select action**, choose **Select All** and then choose **Add statement**.

5. Repeat the preceding step for each of the following services: **Amazon S3**, **Elastic Load Balancing**, **AWS CodeCommit**, **AWS CloudTrail**, and **AWS CodeDeploy**.

   Choose **Select All** for the actions for each service, and then choose **Add another statement**.

6. When you are done, choose **Create policy** to save the SCP.

7. Choose the new policy in the list and then choose **Policy editor** to view the new policy's JSON content. It looks similar to the following (shown here with some formatting compressed to save space):

```
1  {
2      "Version": "2012-10-17",
3      "Statement": [
4          {
5              "Sid": "Stmt1111111111111",
6              "Effect": "Allow",
7              "Action": [ "ec2:*" ],
8              "Resource": [ "*" ]
9          },
10         {
11             "Sid": "Stmt2222222222222",
12             "Effect": "Allow",
13             "Action": [ "s3:*" ],
14             "Resource": [ "*" ]
15         },
16         {
17             "Sid": "Stmt3333333333333",
18             "Effect": "Allow",
19             "Action": [ "elasticloadbalancing:*" ],
20             "Resource": [ "*" ]
21         },
22         {
23             "Sid": "Stmt4444444444444",
24             "Effect": "Allow",
25             "Action": [ "codecommit:*" ],
26             "Resource": [ "*" ]
27         },
28         {
29             "Sid": "Stmt5555555555555",
30             "Effect": "Allow",
31             "Action": [ "cloudtrail:*" ],
32             "Resource": [ "*" ]
```

```
33        },
34        {
35             "Sid": "Stmt6666666666666",
36             "Effect": "Allow",
37             "Action": [ "codedeploy:*" ],
38             "Resource": [ "*" ]
39        }
40    ]
41 }
```

The final policy provides a blacklist of services that are blocked from use in the MainApp OU. For this tutorial, you block access to Amazon DynamoDB in any accounts that are in the MainApp OU.

To create the third policy that blacklists services that can't be used in the MainApp OU

1. Choose **All policies** at the top of the page to go back to the list, choose **Create policy**, and then choose **Policy generator**.

2. For **Policy name**, type **Blacklist for MainApp Prohibited Services**.

3. For **Choose Overall Effect**, choose **Deny**.

4. In the **Statement builder**, select **Amazon DynamoDB**. For **Select action**, choose **Select All** and then choose **Add another statement**.

5. Choose **Create policy** to save the SCP.

6. Choose the new policy in the list, and then choose **Policy editor** to view the new policy's JSON content. It looks similar to the following (shown here with some formatting compressed to save space):

```
1 {
2    "Version": "2012-10-17",
3    "Statement": [
4      {
5        "Effect": "Deny",
6        "Action": [ "dynamodb:*" ],
7        "Resource": [ "*" ]
8      }
9    ]
10 }
```

Enable the Service Control Policy Type in the Root

Before you can attach a policy of any type to a root or to any OU within a root, you must enable the policy type for that root. Policy types are not enabled in any root by default. The steps in this section show you how to enable the service control policy (SCP) type for the root in your organization.

Note
Currently, you can have only one root in your organization. It's created for you and named **Root** when you create your organization.

To enable SCPs for your root

1. On the **Organize accounts** tab, choose your root.

2. In the Details pane on the right, under **ENABLE/DISABLE POLICY TYPES** and next to **Service control policies**, choose **Enable**.

Attach the SCPs to Your OUs

Now that the SCPs exist and are enabled for your root, you can attach them to the root and OUs.

To attach the policies to the root and the OUs

1. Still on the **Organize accounts** tab, in the Details pane on the right, under **POLICIES**, choose **SERVICE CONTROL POLICIES**.

2. Choose **Attach** next to the SCP named `Block CloudTrail Configuration Actions` to prevent anyone from altering the way that you configured CloudTrail. In this tutorial, you attach it to the root so that it affects all member accounts.

   The Details pane now shows by highlighting that two SCPs are attached to the root: the one you just created and the default `FullAWSAccess` SCP.

3. Choose the **Production** OU (not the check box) to navigate to its contents.

4. Under **POLICIES**, choose **SERVICE CONTROL POLICIES**, and then choose **Attach** next to `Whitelist for All Approved Services` to enable users or roles in member accounts in the Production OU to access the approved services.

5. The information pane now shows that two SCPs are attached to the OU: the one that you just attached and the default `FullAWSAccess` SCP. However, because the `FullAWSAccess` SCP is also a whitelist that allows all services and actions, you must detach this SCP to ensure that only your approved services are allowed.

6. To remove the default policy from the Production OU, next to **FullAWSAccess**, choose **Detach**. After you remove this default policy, all member accounts under the root immediately lose access to all actions and services that are not on the whitelist SCP that you attached in the preceding step. Even if an administrator in one of the accounts grants full access to another service by attaching an AWS Identity and Access Management (IAM) permission policy to a user in one of the member accounts, any requests to use actions that aren't included in the **Whitelist for All Approved Services** SCP are denied.

7. Now you can attach the SCP named `Blacklist for MainApp Prohibited services` to prevent anyone in the accounts in the MainApp OU from using any of the restricted services.

   To do this, choose the **MainApp** OU (not the check box) to navigate to its contents.

8. In the Details pane, under **POLICIES**, expand the **Service control policies** section. In the list of available policies, next to **Blacklist for MainApp Prohibited Services**, choose **Attach**.

Step 4: Testing Your Organization's Policies

You now can sign in as a user in any of the member accounts and try to perform various AWS actions:

- If you sign in as a user in the master account, you can perform any operation that is allowed by your IAM permission policies. The SCPs don't affect any user or role in the master account, no matter which root or OU the account is located in.
- If you sign in as the root user or an IAM user in account 222222222222, you can perform any actions that are allowed by the whitelist. AWS Organizations denies any attempt to perform an action in any service that isn't in the whitelist. Also, AWS Organizations denies any attempt to perform one of the CloudTrail configuration actions.
- If you sign in as a user in account 333333333333, you can perform any actions that are allowed by the whitelist and not blocked by the blacklist. AWS Organizations denies any attempt to perform an action that isn't in the whitelist policy and any action that is in the blacklist policy. Also, AWS Organizations denies any attempt to perform one of the CloudTrail configuration actions.

Tutorial: Monitor Important Changes to Your Organization with CloudWatch Events

This tutorial shows how to configure CloudWatch Events to monitor your organization for changes. You start by configuring a rule that is triggered when users invoke specific Organizations operations. Next, you configure CloudWatch Events to run an AWS Lambda function when the rule is triggered, and you configure Amazon SNS to send an email with details about the event.

The following illustration shows the main steps of the tutorial.

Step 1: Configure a Trail and Event Selector
Create a log, called a *trail*, in AWS CloudTrail. You configure it to capture all API calls.

Step 2: Configure a Lambda Function
Create an AWS Lambda function that logs details about the event to an S3 bucket.

Step 3: Create an Amazon SNS Topic That Sends Emails to Subscribers
Create an Amazon SNS topic that sends emails to its subscribers, and then subscribe yourself to the topic.

Step 4: Create a CloudWatch Events Rule
Create a rule that tells CloudWatch Events to pass details of specified API calls to the Lambda function and to SNS topic subscribers.

Step 5: Test Your CloudWatch Events Rule
Test your new rule by running one of the monitored operations. In this tutorial, the monitored operation is creating an organizational unit (OU). You view the log entry that the Lambda function creates, and you view the email that Amazon SNS sends to subscribers.

Prerequisites

This tutorial assumes the following:

- You can sign in to the AWS Management Console as an IAM user from the master account in your organization. The IAM user must have permissions to create and configure a log in CloudTrail, a function in Lambda, a topic in Amazon SNS, and a rule in CloudWatch. For more information about granting permissions, see Access Management in the *IAM User Guide*, or the guide for the service for which you want to configure access.
- You have access to an existing Amazon Simple Storage Service (Amazon S3) bucket (or you have permissions to create a bucket) to receive the CloudTrail log that you configure in step 1.

Important
Currently, AWS Organizations is hosted in only the US East (N. Virginia) Region (even though it is available globally). To perform the steps in this tutorial, you must configure the AWS Management Console to use that region.

Step 1: Configure a Trail and Event Selector

In this step, you sign in to the master account and configure a log (called a *trail*) in AWS CloudTrail. You also configure an event selector on the trail to capture all read/write API calls so that CloudWatch Events has calls to trigger on.

To create a trail

1. Sign in to AWS as an administrator of the organization's master account and then open the CloudTrail console at https://console.aws.amazon.com/cloudtrail/.

2. On the navigation bar in the upper-right corner of the console, choose the **US East (N. Virginia)** Region. If you choose a different region, AWS Organizations doesn't appear as an option in the CloudWatch Events configuration settings, and CloudTrail doesn't capture information about Organizations.

3. In the navigation pane, choose **Trails**.

4. Choose **Add new trail**.

5. For **Trail name**, type **My-Test-Trail**.

6. Perform one of the following options to specify where CloudTrail is to deliver its logs:

   - If you already have a bucket, choose **No** next to **Create a new S3 bucket** and then choose the bucket name from the **S3 bucket** list.
   - If you need to create a bucket, choose **Yes** next to **Create a new S3 bucket** and then, for **S3 bucket**, type a name for the new bucket. **Note**
     S3 bucket names must be *globally* unique.

7. Choose **Create**.

8. Choose the trail My-Test-Trail that you just created.

9. Choose the pencil icon next to **Management events**.

10. For **Read/Write events**, choose **All**, choose **Save**, and then choose **Configure**.

CloudWatch Events enables you to choose from several different ways to send alerts when an alarm rule matches an incoming API call. This tutorial demonstrates two methods: invoking a Lambda function that can log the API call and sending information to an Amazon SNS topic that sends an email or text message to the topic's subscribers. In the next two steps, you create the components you need, the Lambda function, and the Amazon SNS topic.

Step 2: Configure a Lambda Function

In this step, you create a Lambda function that logs the API activity that is sent to it by the CloudWatch Events rule that you configure later.

To create a Lambda function that logs CloudWatch Events events

1. Open the AWS Lambda console at https://console.aws.amazon.com/lambda/.

2. If you are new to Lambda, choose **Get Started Now** on the welcome page; otherwise, choose **Create a Lambda function**.

3. On the **Select blueprint** page, type **hello** for the filter, and then choose the **hello-world** blueprint.

4. On the **Configure triggers** page, choose **Next**.

5. On the **Configure function** page, do the following:

   1. For the Lambda function name, type **LogOrganizationEvents**.

   2. Edit the code for the Lambda function, as shown in the following example:

```
1 'use strict';
2
3 exports.handler = (event, context, callback) => {
4     console.log('LogOrganizationEvents');
5     console.log('Received event:', JSON.stringify(event, null, 2));
6     callback(null, 'Finished');
7 };
```

This sample code logs the event with a **LogOrganizationEvents** marker string followed by the JSON string that makes up the event.

6. For **Role**, choose **Create a custom role** and then, at the bottom of the **AWS Lambda requires access to your resources** page, choose **Allow**. This role grants your Lambda function permissions to access the data it requires and to write its output log.

7. At the bottom of the page, choose **Next**.

8. On the **Review** page, verify your selections and choose **Create function**.

Step 3: Create an Amazon SNS Topic That Sends Emails to Subscribers

In this step, you create an Amazon SNS topic that emails information to its subscribers. You make this topic a "target" of the CloudWatch Events rule that you create later.

To create an Amazon SNS topic to send an email to subscribers

1. Open the Amazon SNS console at https://console.aws.amazon.com/sns/.

2. In the navigation pane, choose **Topics**.

3. Choose **Create new topic**.

   1. For **Topic name**, type **OrganizationsCloudWatchTopic**.

   2. For **Display name**, type **OrgsCWEvnt**.

   3. Choose **Create topic**.

4. Now you can create a subscription for the topic. Choose the ARN for the topic that you just created.

5. Choose **Create subscription**.

   1. On the **Create subscription** page, for **Protocol**, choose **Email**.

   2. For **Endpoint**, type your email address.

   3. Choose **Create subscription**. AWS sends an email to the email address that you specified in the preceding step. Wait for that email to arrive, and then choose the **Confirm subscription** link in the email to verify that you successfully received the email.

   4. Return to the console and refresh the page. The **Pending confirmation** message disappears and is replaced by the now valid subscription ID.

Step 4: Create a CloudWatch Events Rule

Now that the required Lambda function exists in your account, you create a CloudWatch Events rule that invokes it when the criteria in the rule are met.

To create a CloudWatch Events rule

1. Open the CloudWatch console at https://console.aws.amazon.com/cloudwatch/.

2. In the navigation pane, choose **Events**, and then choose **Create rule**.

3. For **Event source**, do the following:

   1. Choose **Event pattern**.

   2. Choose **Build event pattern to match events by service**.

   3. For **Service Name**, choose **Organizations**.

   4. For **Event Type**, choose **AWS API Call via CloudTrail**.

5. Choose **Specific operation(s)**, and then enter the APIs that you want monitored: **CreateAccount**, **CreateOrganizationalUnit**, and **LeaveOrganization**. You can select any others that you also want. For a complete list of available AWS Organizations APIs, see the AWS Organizations API Reference.

4. Under **Targets**, under **Lambda function**, in the drop-down list, select the function you created in the previous procedure.

5. Under **Targets**, choose **Add target**.

6. In the new target row, choose the drop-down header, and then choose **SNS topic**.

7. For **Topic**, choose the topic named **OrganizationCloudWatchTopic** that you created in the preceding procedure.

8. Choose **Configure details**.

9. On the **Configure rule details** page, for **Name** type **OrgsMonitorRule**, leave **State** selected and then choose **Create rule**.

Step 5: Test Your CloudWatch Events Rule

In this step, you create an organizational unit (OU) and observe the CloudWatch Events rule generate a log entry and send an email to you with details about the event.

To create an OU

1. Open the AWS Organizations console at https://console.aws.amazon.com/organizations/.

2. Choose the **Organize Accounts** tab, and then choose **Create organizational unit**.

3. For the name of the OU, type **TestCWEOU**, and then choose **Create organizational unit**.

To see the CloudWatch Events log entry

1. Open the CloudWatch console at https://console.aws.amazon.com/cloudwatch/.

2. In the navigation page, choose **Logs**.

3. On the **Log Groups** page, choose the group that is associated with your Lambda function: **/aws/lambda/LogOrganizationEvents**.

4. Each group contains one or more streams, and there should be one group for today. Choose it.

5. View the log. You should see rows similar to the following:

```
  22:45:05          2017-03-09T22:45:05.099Z 0999eb20-051a-11e7-a426-cddb46425f16 LogOrganizationEvents
  22:45:05          2017-03-09T22:45:05.101Z 0999eb20-051a-11e7-a426-cddb46425f16 Received event: { "version": "0", "id": "ca9fc4e
  22:45:05          END RequestId: 0999eb20-051a-11e7-a426-cddb46425f16
```

6. Select the middle row of the entry to see the full JSON text of the received event. You can see all the details of the API request in the `requestParameters` and `responseElements` pieces of the output:

```
1  2017-03-09T22:45:05.101Z 0999eb20-051a-11e7-a426-cddb46425f16 Received event:
2  {
3      "version": "0",
4      "id": "123456-EXAMPLE-GUID-123456",
5      "detail-type": "AWS API Call via CloudTrail",
6      "source": "aws.organizations",
7      "account": "123456789012",
8      "time": "2017-03-09T22:44:26Z",
9      "region": "us-east-1",
10     "resources": [],
```

```
11      "detail": {
12          "eventVersion": "1.04",
13          "userIdentity": {
14              ...
15          },
16          "eventTime": "2017-03-09T22:44:26Z",
17          "eventSource": "organizations.amazonaws.com",
18          "eventName": "CreateOrganizationalUnit",
19          "awsRegion": "us-east-1",
20          "sourceIPAddress": "192.168.0.1",
21          "userAgent": "AWS Organizations Console, aws-internal/3",
22          "requestParameters": {
23              "parentId": "r-exampleRootId",
24              "name": "TestCWEOU"
25          },
26          "responseElements": {
27              "organizationalUnit": {
28                  "name": "TestCWEOU",
29                  "id": "ou-exampleRootId-exampleOUId",
30                  "arn": "arn:aws:organizations::1234567789012:ou/o-exampleOrgId/ou-
                        exampleRootId-exampeOUId"
31              }
32          },
33          "requestID": "123456-EXAMPLE-GUID-123456",
34          "eventID": "123456-EXAMPLE-GUID-123456",
35          "eventType": "AwsApiCall"
36      }
37 }
```

7. Check your email account for a message from **OrgsCWEvnt** (the display name of your Amazon SNS topic). The body of the email contains the same JSON text output as the log entry that is shown in the preceding step.

Clean up: Remove the Resources You No Longer Need

To avoid incurring charges, you should delete any AWS resources that you created as part of this tutorial that you don't want to keep.

To clean up your AWS environment

1. Use the CloudTrail console at https://console.aws.amazon.com/cloudtrail/ to delete the trail named **My-Test-Trail** that you created in step 1.

2. If you created an Amazon S3 bucket in step 1, use the Amazon S3 console at https://console.aws.amazon.com/s3/ to delete it.

3. Use the Lambda console at https://console.aws.amazon.com/lambda/ to delete the function named **LogOrganizationEvents** that you created in step 2.

4. Use the Amazon SNS console at https://console.aws.amazon.com/sns/ to delete the Amazon SNS topic named **OrganizationsCloudWatchTopic** that you created in step 3.

5. Use the CloudWatch console at https://console.aws.amazon.com/cloudwatch/ to delete the CloudWatch rule named **OrgsMonitorRule** that you created in step 4.

That's it. In this tutorial, you configured CloudWatch Events to monitor your organization for changes. You configured a rule that is triggered when users invoke specific AWS Organizations operations. The rule ran a

26

Lambda function that logged the event and sent an email that contains details about the event.

Creating and Managing an AWS Organization

You can perform the following tasks using the AWS Organizations console:

- **Create an organization**. Create your organization with your current account as its master account. Create member accounts within your organization, and invite other accounts to join your organization.
- **Enable all features in your organization**. You must enable all features to use the advanced features available in AWS Organizations, such as policies that enable you to apply fine-grained control over which services and actions that member accounts can access. **Note**

  You can also choose to create your organization with only consolidated billing features enabled.
- **View details about your organization**. View details about your organization and its roots, organizational units (OUs), and accounts.
- **Delete an organization**. Delete an organization when you no longer need it.

Note

The procedures in this section specify the minimum permissions needed to perform the tasks. These typically apply to the API or access to the command line tool.

Performing a task in the console might require additional permissions. For example, you could grant read-only permissions to all users in your organization, and then grant other permissions that allow select users to perform specific tasks. For an example of a policy that grants read-only permissions to an organization, see Granting Limited Access by Actions.

Creating an Organization

You can use AWS Organizations to create your own organization to consolidate and manage your AWS accounts.

You can create an organization that starts with your AWS account as the master account. After you sign in to your account, you can create other AWS accounts that automatically are added to your organization as member accounts. You also can invite existing AWS accounts to join as member accounts. When you create an organization, you can choose whether the organization supports all features or only consolidated billing features.

Minimum permissions
To create an organization with your current AWS account, you must have the following permissions:
`organizations:CreateOrganization`

To create an organization (Console)

1. Sign in to the AWS Management Console and open the AWS Organizations console at https://console.aws. amazon.com/organizations/. You must sign in as an IAM user, assume an IAM role, or sign in as the root user (not recommended) in the account that you want to be the organization's master account.

2. On the introduction page, choose **Create organization**.

3. Choose whether to create the organization with only consolidated billing features or with all features enabled.

4. In the **Create organization** confirmation dialog box, choose **Create organization**.

5. Choose the **Accounts** tab. The star next to the account email indicates that it is the master account.

6. From here you can do the following:

   - Follow the steps in Inviting an AWS Account to Join Your Organization to invite other accounts to join your organization. If the invited account accepts your invitation, the account appears on the AWS Organizations console.
   - Follow the steps in Creating an AWS Account in Your Organization to create an AWS account that automatically is part of your AWS organization.

To create an organization (AWS CLI, AWS API)
You can use one of the following commands to create an organization:

- AWS CLI: aws organizations create-organization
- AWS API: CreateOrganization

Enabling All Features in Your Organization

AWS Organizations has two available feature sets: consolidated billing features and all features. All organizations support consolidated billing, which provides basic management tools that you can use to centrally manage the accounts in your organization. If you enable all features, you continue to get all the consolidated billing features plus a set of advanced features such as service control policies (SCPs), which give you fine-grained control over which services and actions that member accounts can access.

When you start the process to enable all features, AWS Organizations sends a request to every member account that you *invited* to join your organization. Every invited account must approve enabling all features by accepting the request. Only then can you complete the process to enable all features in your organization. If an account declines the request, you must either remove the account from your organization or resend the request and get it accepted before you can complete the process to enable all features. Accounts that you *created* using AWS Organizations don't get a request because they don't need to approve the additional control.

Organizations also verifies that every account has a service-linked role named `AWSServiceRoleForOrganizations`. This role is mandatory in all accounts to enable all features. If you deleted the role in an invited account, accepting the invitation to enable all features recreates the role. If you deleted the role in an account that was created using AWS Organizations, that account receives an invitation specifically to recreate that role. All of these invitations must be accepted for the organization to complete the process of enabling all features.

Notes
Currently, AWS Organizations offers only one type of policy called a SCP. Currently, you can have only one root in your organization. While enabling all features is in progress, you can't invite accounts to join the organization. You must wait until the process to enable all features is complete. Alternatively, you can cancel the process to enable all features, invite the accounts, and then restart the process to enable all features. While enabling all features is in progress, you can continue to create accounts within the organization.

After you enable all features in your organization, you can enable support in the root for one or more policy types, such as SCPs. Within the root, you can attach the policies of the enabled types to the roots, OUs, and accounts in your organization. For more information, see Managing Organization Policies.

Important
After you enable all features in your organization, the master account in the organization can apply policies to all member accounts.
An SCP can restrict what users and even administrators can do in affected accounts. The master account can apply SCPs that can prevent member accounts from leaving the organization. Ensure that your account administrators are aware of this. The migration from consolidated billing features to all features is one-way. You can't switch an organization with all features enabled back to consolidated billing features only. The master account is not affected by any SCP. You can't limit what users and roles in the master account can do by applying SCPs. SCPs affect only member accounts.

If your organization has only consolidated billing features enabled, then member account administrators can choose to delete the service-linked role named `AWSServiceRoleForOrganizations`. However, when you enable all features in an organization, this role is required and is recreated in all accounts as part of accepting the invitation to enable all features. For more information about how AWS Organizations uses this role, see AWS Organizations and Service-Linked Roles.

Beginning the Process to Enable All Features

When you sign in with permissions to your organization's master account, you can begin the process to enable all features. To do this, complete the following steps.

Minimum permissions
To enable all features in your organization, you must have the following permission:
`organizations:EnableAllFeatures`

To ask your member accounts to agree to enable all features in the organization

1. Sign in to the AWS Management Console and open the AWS Organizations console at https://console.aws.amazon.com/organizations/. You must sign in as an IAM user, assume an IAM role, or sign in as the root user (not recommended) in the organization's master account.

2. On the **Settings** tab, choose **Begin process to enable all features**.

3. Acknowledge your understanding that you cannot return to only consolidated billing features after you switch by choosing **Begin process to enable all features**. AWS Organizations sends a request to every invited (not created) account in the organization asking for approval to enable all features in the organization. If you have any accounts that were created using AWS Organizations and the member account administrator deleted the service-linked role named `AWSServiceRoleForOrganizations`, AWS Organizations sends that account a request to recreate the role.

4. To view the status of the requests, choose **View all feature request approval status**.

    The **All feature request approval status** page shows the current request status for each account in the organization. Accounts that have agreed to the request have a green check mark and show the **Acceptance** date. Accounts that haven't yet agreed have a yellow exclamation point icon and show the date that the request was sent with a status of **Open**. **Note**
    A countdown of 90 days begins when the request is sent to the member accounts. All accounts must approve the request within that time period or the request expires. All requests related to this attempt are canceled, and you have to start over with step 2. During the time between when you make the request to enable all features and when either all accounts accept or the timeout occurs, all pending invitations for other accounts to join the organization are automatically canceled. You can't issue new invitations until the process of enabling all features is finished. After you complete the process of enabling all features, you once again can invite accounts to join the organization. The process doesn't change, but all invitations include information letting the recipients know that if they accept the invitation, they're subject to any applicable policies.

5. If an account doesn't approve its request, you can select the account in the **Account progress** page, and then choose **Remove**. This cancels the request for the selected account and removes that account from the organization, eliminating the blocker to enabling all features.

6. After all accounts approve the requests, you can finalize the process and enable all features. You can also immediately finalize the process if your organization doesn't have any invited member accounts. Finalizing the process requires only a couple of clicks in the console. See Finalizing the Process to Enable All Features.

To ask your invited member accounts to agree to enable all features in the organization (AWS CLI, AWS API)
You can use one of the following commands to enable all features in an organization:

- AWS CLI: aws organizations enable-all-features
- AWS API: EnableAllFeatures

Approving the Request to Enable All Features or to Recreate the Service-Linked Role

When signed in with permissions to one of the organization's invited member accounts, you can approve a request from the master account. If your account was originally invited to join the organization, the invitation is to enable all features and implicitly includes approval for recreating the `AWSServiceRoleForOrganizations` role, if needed. If your account was instead created using AWS Organizations and you deleted the `AWSServiceRoleForOrganizations` service-linked role, you receive an invitation only to recreate the role. To do this, complete the following steps.

Minimum permissions
To approve a request to enable all features for your member account, you must have the following permissions:

`organizations:AcceptHandshake` `iam:CreateServiceLinkedRole` – Required only if the `AWSServiceRoleForOrganizations` role must be recreated in the member account

Important

If you perform the steps in the following procedure, the master account in the organization can apply policy-based controls on your member account that can restrict what users and even what you as the administrator can do in your account. Additionally, the master account can apply a policy that might prevent your account from leaving the organization.

To agree to the request to enable all features in the organization (console)

1. Sign in to the AWS Management Console and open the AWS Organizations console at https://console.aws. amazon.com/organizations/. You must sign in as an IAM user, assume an IAM role, or sign in as the root user (not recommended) in the organization's master account.

2. Read what accepting the request for all features in the organization means for your account, and then choose **Accept**. The page continues to show the process as incomplete until all accounts in the organization accept the requests and the administrator of the master account finalizes the process.

To agree to the request to enable all features in the organization (AWS CLI, AWS API)
To agree to the request, you must accept the handshake with `"Action": "APPROVE_ALL_FEATURES"`.

- AWS CLI: aws organizations accept-handshake
- AWS API: AcceptHandshake

Finalizing the Process to Enable All Features

After all invited member accounts must approve the request to enable all features. If there are no invited member accounts in the organization, the **Enable all features progress** page indicates with a green banner that you can finalize the process.

Minimum permissions
To finalize the process to enable all features for the organization, you must have the following permission:
`organizations:AcceptHandshake`

To finalize the process to enable all features (console)

1. Sign in to the AWS Management Console and open the AWS Organizations console at https://console.aws. amazon.com/organizations/. You must sign in as an IAM user, assume an IAM role, or sign in as the root user (not recommended) in the organization's master account.

2. On the **Settings** tab, under **ENABLE ALL FEATURES**, choose **View all feature request approval status**.

3. After all accounts accept the request to enable all features, in the green box at the top of the page, choose **Finalize process to enable all features** and then, in the confirmation dialog box, choose **Finalize process to enable all features** again.

4. The organization now has all features enabled. The next step is to enable the policy types that you want to use. For more information, see Enabling and Disabling a Policy Type on a Root. After that, you can attach policies to administer the accounts in your organization. For more information, see Attaching a Policy to Roots, OUs, or Accounts

To finalize the process to enable all features (AWS CLI, AWS API)
To finalize the process, you must accept the handshake with `"Action": "ENABLE_ALL_FEATURES"`.

- AWS CLI: aws organizations accept-handshake
- AWS API: AcceptHandshake

Viewing Details About Your Organization

You can perform the following tasks using the AWS Organizations console:

- Viewing Details of an Organization from the Master Account
- Viewing Details of a Root
- Viewing Details of an OU
- Viewing Details of an Account

Viewing Details of an Organization from the Master Account

Minimum permissions

To view the details of an organization, you must have the following permission:
`organizations:DescribeOrganization`

To view details of an organization (console)

When signed in to the organization's master account in the AWS Organizations console, you can view details of the organization.

1. Sign in to the Organizations console at https://console.aws.amazon.com/organizations/. You must sign in as an IAM user, assume an IAM role, or sign in as the root user (not recommended) in the organization's master account.

2. Choose the **Settings** tab.

   The console displays details about the organization, including its ID, its ARN, and the email address of the owner of its master account.

To view details of an organization (AWS CLI, AWS API)

You can use one of the following commands to view details of an organization:

- AWS CLI: aws organizations describe-organization
- AWS API: DescribeOrganization

Viewing Details of a Root

Minimum permissions

To view the details of a root, you must have the following permissions:
`organizations:DescribeOrganization` (console only) `organizations:ListRoots`

To view details of a root (console)

When signed in to the organization's master account in the AWS Organizations console, you can view details of a root.

1. Sign in to the Organizations console at https://console.aws.amazon.com/organizations/. You must sign in as an IAM user, assume an IAM role, or sign in as the root user (not recommended) in the organization's master account.

2. Choose the **Organize accounts** tab, and then choose **Home**.

3. Choose the **Root** entity. Root is the default name, but you can rename it using the API or command line tools.

   The **Root** pane on the right side of the page shows the details of the root.

To view details of a root (AWS CLI, AWS API)

You can use one of the following commands to view details of a root:

- AWS CLI: aws organizations list-roots
- AWS API: ListRoots

Viewing Details of an OU

Minimum permissions
To view the details of an organizational unit (OU), you must have the following permissions:
`organizations:DescribeOrganizationalUnit` `organizations:DescribeOrganization` (console only)
`organizations:ListOrganizationsUnitsForParent` (console only) `organizations:ListRoots` (console only)

To view details of an OU (console)

When signed in to the organization's master account in the AWS Organizations console, you can view details of the OUs in your organization.

1. Sign in to the Organizations console at https://console.aws.amazon.com/organizations/. You must sign in as an IAM user, assume an IAM role, or sign in as the root user (not recommended) in the organization's master account.

2. On the **Organize accounts** tab, navigate to the OU that you want to examine. If the OU that you want is a child of another OU, choose each OU in the hierarchy to find the one you're looking for.

3. Select the check box for the OU.

   The Details pane on the right side of the page shows information about the OU.

To view details of an OU (AWS CLI, AWS API)
You can use one of the following commands to view details of an OU:

- AWS CLI: aws organizations describe-organizational-unit
- AWS API: DescribeOrganizationalUnit

Viewing Details of an Account

Minimum permissions
To view the details of an AWS account, you must have the following permissions:
`organizations:DescribeAccount` `organizations:DescribeOrganization` (console only) `organizations:ListAccounts` (console only)

To view details of an AWS account (console)

When signed in to the organization's master account in the AWS Organizations console, you can view details about your accounts.

1. Sign in to the Organizations console at https://console.aws.amazon.com/organizations/. You must sign in as an IAM user, assume an IAM role, or sign in as the root user (not recommended) in the organization's master account.

2. Do one of the following:

   - On the **Accounts** tab, choose the account that you want to examine.
   - On the **Organize accounts** tab, navigate to and then choose an account card.

   The **Account summary** pane on the right side of the page shows details of the selected account.

Note
By default, failed account creation requests are hidden on the **Accounts** tab. You can include them in the list by choosing the switch at the top to change it to **Show**.

To view details of an account (AWS CLI, AWS API)
You can use one of the following commands to view details of an account:

- AWS CLI: aws organizations describe-account
- AWS API: DescribeAccount

Remove the Master Account and Delete the Organization

When you no longer need your organization, you can delete it. This removes the master account from the organization and deletes the organization itself. The former master account becomes a standalone AWS account. You then have three options: You can continue to use it as a standalone account, you can use it to create a different organization, or you can accept an invitation from another organization to add the account to that organization as a member account.

Important

If you delete an organization, you will not be able to recover it. If you created any policies inside of the organization, they will also be deleted. You can delete an organization only after you remove all member accounts from the organization. If you created some of your member accounts using AWS Organizations, you might be blocked from removing those accounts. You can remove a member account only if it has all the information that is required to operate as a standalone AWS account. For more information about how to provide that information and remove the account, see Leaving an Organization as a Member Account.

When you remove the master account from an organization by deleting the organization, the account is affected in the following ways:

- The account is responsible for paying only its own charges and is no longer responsible for the charges incurred by any other account.
- Integration with other services might be disabled. For example, AWS Single Sign-On requires an organization to operate, so if you remove an account from an organization that supports AWS SSO, the users in that account can no longer use that service.

The master account of an organization is never affected by service control policies (SCPs), so there is no change in permissions after SCPs are no longer available.

To remove the master account from an organization and delete the organization (console) Minimum permissions

To delete an organization, you must sign in as an IAM user or role in the master account, and you must have the following permissions:

`organizations:DeleteOrganization organizations:DescribeOrganization` (console only)

1. Sign in to the Organizations console at https://console.aws.amazon.com/organizations/. You must sign in as an IAM user, assume an IAM role, or sign in as the root user (not recommended) in the organization's master account.

2. Before you can delete the organization, you must first remove all accounts from the organization. For more information, see Removing a Member Account from Your Organization.

3. On the **Settings** tab, choose **Delete organization**.

4. In the **Delete organization** confirmation dialog box, choose **Delete organization**.

5. (Optional) If you also want to close this account, you can follow the steps at Closing an AWS Account.

To delete an organization (AWS CLI, AWS API)

You can use one of the following commands to delete an organization:

- AWS CLI: aws organizations delete-organization
- AWS API: DeleteOrganization

Managing the AWS Accounts in Your Organization

An organization is a collection of AWS accounts that you centrally manage. You can perform the following tasks to manage the accounts that are part of your organization:

- View details of the accounts in your organization. You can see the account's unique ID number, its Amazon Resource Name (ARN), and the policies that are attached to it.
- Invite existing AWS accounts to join your organization. Create invitations, manage invitations that you have created, and accept or decline invitations.
- Create an AWS account as part of your organization. Create and access an AWS account that is automatically part of your organization.
- Remove an AWS account from your organization. As an administrator in the master account, remove member accounts that you no longer want to manage from your organization. As an administrator of a member account, remove your account from its organization. If the master account has attached a policy to your member account, you could be blocked from removing your account.
- Delete (or close) an AWS account. When you no longer need an AWS account, you can close the account to prevent any usage or accrual of charges.

Impact on an AWS Account That You Invite to Join an Organization

When you invite an AWS account to join an organization and the owner of the account accepts the invitation, AWS Organizations automatically makes the following changes to the new member account:

- AWS Organizations creates a service-linked role called AWSServiceRoleForOrganizations. The account must have this role if your organization supports all features. You can delete the role if the organization supports only the consolidated billing feature set. If you delete the role and later you enable all features in your organization, AWS Organizations recreates the role for the account.
- If you have any service control policies (SCPs) attached to the root of the OU tree, those SCPs immediately apply to all users and roles in the invited account. AWS Organizations adds new accounts to the root OU by default.
- If you have enabled service trust for another AWS service for your organization, that trusted service can create service-linked roles or perform actions in any member account in the organization, including an invited account.

For invited member accounts, AWS Organizations doesn't automatically create the IAM role OrganizationAccountAccessRole. This role grants the master account administrative control of the member account. If you want to enable that level of administrative control, you can manually add the role to the invited account. For more information, see Creating the OrganizationAccountAccessRole in an Invited Member Account.

If you invite an account to join an organization that has only the consolidated billing features enabled and you later want to enable all features for the organization, invited accounts must approve the change.

Impact on an AWS Account That You Create in an Organization

When you create an AWS account in your organization, AWS Organizations automatically makes the following changes to the new member account:

- AWS Organizations creates a service-linked role called AWSServiceRoleForOrganizations. The account must have this role if your organization supports all features. You can delete the role if the organization supports only the consolidated billing feature set. If you delete the role and later you enable all features in your organization, AWS Organizations recreates the role for the account.
- AWS Organizations creates the IAM role OrganizationAccountAccessRole. This role grants the master account access to the new member account. This role can be deleted.
- If you have any SCPs attached to the root of the OU tree, those SCPs immediately apply to all users and roles in the created account. New accounts are added to the root OU by default.

- If you have enabled service trust for another AWS service for your organization, that trusted service can create service-linked roles or perform actions in any member account in the organization, including your created account.

Inviting an AWS Account to Join Your Organization

You can invite existing AWS accounts to join your organization. When you start this process, AWS Organizations sends an invitation to the account owner, who then decides whether to accept or decline the invitation. You can use the AWS Organizations console to initiate and manage invitations that you send to other accounts. You can send an invitation to another account only from the master account of your organization.

If you are the administrator of an AWS account, you also can accept or decline an invitation from an organization. If you accept, your account becomes a member of that organization. Your account can join only one organization, so if you receive multiple invitations to join, you can accept only one.

- Sending Invitations to AWS Accounts
- Managing Pending Invitations for Your Organization
- Accepting or Declining an Invitation from an Organization

When an invited account joins your organization, you *do not* automatically have full administrator control over the account, unlike created accounts. If you want the master account to have full administrative control over an invited member account, you must create the `OrganizationAccountAccessRole` IAM role in the member account and grant permission to the master account to assume the role. To configure this, after the invited account becomes a member, follow the steps in Creating the OrganizationAccountAccessRole in an Invited Member Account.

Note
When you create an account in your organization instead of inviting an existing account to join your organization, AWS Organizations automatically creates an IAM role (named `OrganizationAccountAccessRole` by default) that you can use to grant users in the master account administrator access to the created account.

AWS Organizations *does* automatically create a service-linked role in invited member accounts to support integration between AWS Organizations and other AWS services. For more information, see AWS Organizations and Service-Linked Roles.

You can send up to 20 invitations per day per organization. Each invitation must be responded to within 15 days or it expires.

An invitation that is sent to an account counts against the limit of accounts in your organization. The count is returned if the invited account declines, the master account cancels the invitation, or the invitation expires.

To create an account that automatically is part of your organization, see Creating an AWS Account in Your Organization.

Important
Because of legal and billing constraints, you can invite AWS accounts only from the same AWS seller as the master account. You can't mix accounts from AWS, Amazon Internet Services Pvt. Ltd (AISPL, an AWS seller in India), or Amazon Connect Technology Services (Beijing) Co. (ACTS, an AWS seller in China) in the same organization. You can add accounts from an AWS seller only to an organization with accounts from the same AWS seller.

Sending Invitations to AWS Accounts

When signed in to your organization's master account, you can invite other accounts to join your organization. To do this, complete the following steps.

Minimum permissions
To invite an AWS account to join your organization, you must have the following permissions:
`organizations:DescribeOrganization` (console only) `organizations:InviteAccountToOrganization`

To invite another account to join your organization (console)

1. Sign in to the Organizations console at https://console.aws.amazon.com/organizations/. You must sign in as an IAM user, assume an IAM role, or sign in as the root user (not recommended) in the organization's master account.

2. On the **Accounts** tab, choose **Add account**.

3. Choose **Invite account**.

4. Type either the email address or the account ID number of the AWS account that you want to invite to your organization. If you want to invite multiple accounts, separate them by commas.

5. (Optional) For **Notes**, type any message that you want included in the email invitation to the other account owners.

6. Choose **Invite. Important**
   If you get a message that indicates that you exceeded your account limits for the organization or that you can't add an account because your organization is still initializing, contact AWS Customer Support.

7. The console redirects you to the **Invitations** tab. View all open and accepted invitations on this page. The invitation that you just created appears at the top of the list with its status set to **OPEN**.

   AWS Organizations sends an invitation to the email address of the owner of the account that you invited to the organization. This email includes a link to the AWS Organizations console, where the account owner can view the details and choose to accept or decline the invitation. Alternatively, the owner of the invited account can bypass the email, go directly to the AWS Organizations console, view the invitation, and accept or decline it.

   The invitation to this account immediately counts against the limit to the number of accounts that you can have in your organization; AWS Organizations does not wait until the account accepts the invitation. If the invited account declines, the master account cancels the invitation. If the invited account doesn't respond within the specified time period, the invitation expires. In either case, the invitation no longer counts against your limit.

To invite another account to join your organization (AWS CLI, AWS API)
You can use one of the following commands to invite another account to join your organization:

- AWS CLI: aws organizations invite-account-to-organization
- AWS API: InviteAccountToOrganization

Managing Pending Invitations for Your Organization

When signed in to your master account, you can view all the linked AWS accounts in your organization and cancel any pending (open) invitations. To do this, complete the following steps.

Minimum permissions
To manage pending invitations for your organization, you must have the following permissions:
`organizations:DescribeOrganization` (console only) `organizations:ListHandshakesForOrganization`
`organizations:CancelHandshake`

To view or cancel invitations that are sent from your organization to other accounts (console)

1. Sign in to the Organizations console at https://console.aws.amazon.com/organizations/. You must sign in as an IAM user, assume an IAM role, or sign in as the root user (not recommended) in the organization's master account.

2. Choose the **Invitations** tab. All invitations that are sent from your organization and their current status are listed here. **Note**
   Accepted, canceled, and declined invitations continue to appear in the list for 30 days. After that, they are deleted and no longer appear in the list.

3. For any open invitations that you want to cancel, under the **Actions** column, choose **Cancel**.

   The status of the invitation changes from **Open** to **Canceled**.

   AWS sends an email to the account owner stating that you canceled the invitation. The account can no longer join the organization unless you send a new invitation.

To view or cancel invitations that are sent from your organization to other accounts (AWS CLI, AWS API)

You can use the following commands to view or cancel invitations:

- AWS CLI: aws organizations list-handshakes-for-organization, aws organizations cancel-handshake
- AWS API: ListHandshakesForOrganization, CancelHandshake

Accepting or Declining an Invitation from an Organization

Your AWS account might receive an invitation to join an organization. You can accept or decline the invitation. To do this, complete the following steps.

Minimum permissions

To accept or decline an invitation to join an AWS organization, you must have the following permissions:
`organizations:ListHandshakesForAccount` – Required to see the list of invitations in the AWS Organizations console. `organizations:AcceptHandshake`. `organizations:DeclineHandshake`. `iam:CreateServiceLinkedRole` – Required only when accepting the invitation requires the creation of a service-linked role to support integration with other AWS services. For more information, see AWS Organizations and Service-Linked Roles.

Note

An account's status with an organization affects what cost and usage data is visible:
When a standalone account joins an organization, the account no longer has access to cost and usage data from the time range when the account was a standalone account. If a member account leaves an organization and becomes a standalone account, the account no longer has access to cost and usage data from the time range when the account was a member of the organization. The account has access only to the data that is generated as a standalone account. If a member account leaves organization A to join organization B, the account no longer has access to cost and usage data from the time range when the account was a member of organization A. The account has access only to the data that is generated as a member of organization B. If an account rejoins an organization that it previously belonged to, the account regains access to its historical cost and usage data.

To accept or decline an invitation (console)

1. An invitation to join an organization is sent to the email address of the account owner. If you are an account owner and you receive an invitation email, click the link in the email invitation or go to https://console.aws.amazon.com/organizations/ in your browser, and then choose **Respond to invitations**.

2. If prompted, sign in to the invited account as an IAM user, assume an IAM role, or sign in as the account's root user (not recommended).

3. On the **Invitations** page in the console, you can see your open invitations to join organizations. Choose **Accept** or **Decline**, as appropriate.

   - If you choose **Accept** in the preceding step, in the **Confirm joining the organization** confirmation window, choose **Confirm**.

     The console redirects you to the **Organization overview** page with details about the organization that your account is now a member of. You can view the organization's ID and the owner's email address. **Note**
     Accepted invitations continue to appear in the list for 30 days. After that, they are deleted and no longer appear in the list.

AWS Organizations automatically creates a service-linked role in the new member account to support integration between AWS Organizations and other AWS services. For more information, see AWS Organizations and Service-Linked Roles.

AWS sends an email to the owner of the organization's master account stating that you accepted the invitation. It also sends an email to the member account owner stating that the account is now a member of the organization.

- If you choose **Decline** in the preceding step, your account remains on the **Invitations** page that lists any other pending invitations.

AWS sends an email to the organization's master account owner stating that you declined the invitation.
Note
Declined invitations continue to appear in the list for 30 days. After that, they are deleted and no longer appear in the list.

To accept or decline an invitation (AWS CLI, AWS API)
You can use the following commands to accept or decline an invitation:

- AWS CLI: aws organizations accept-handshake, aws organizations decline-handshake
- AWS API: AcceptHandshake, DeclineHandshake

Creating an AWS Account in Your Organization

An organization is a collection of AWS accounts that you centrally manage. You can perform the following procedures to manage the accounts that are part of your organization:

- Creating an AWS Account That Is Part of Your Organization
- Accessing a Member Account That Has a Master Account Access Role

Important
When you create a member account in your organization, AWS Organizations automatically creates an IAM role in the member account that enables IAM users in the master account to exercise full administrative control over the member account. Note that this role is subject to any service control policies (SCPs) that apply to the member account.
AWS Organizations also automatically creates a service-linked role named `AWSServiceRoleForOrganizations` that enables integration with select AWS services. You must configure the other services to allow the integration. For more information, see AWS Organizations and Service-Linked Roles.

Creating an AWS Account That Is Part of Your Organization

When signed in to the organization's master account, you can create member accounts that are automatically part of your organization. To do this, complete the following steps.

Minimum permissions
To create a member account in your organization, you must have the following permissions:
`organizations:DescribeOrganization` (console only) `organizations:CreateAccount`

Important
When you create an account using the following procedure, AWS doesn't automatically collect all the information required for an account to operate as a standalone account. If you ever need to remove the account from the organization and make it a standalone account, you must provide that information for the account before you can remove it. For more information, see Leaving an Organization as a Member Account.

To create an AWS account that automatically is part of your organization (console)

1. Sign in to the Organizations console at https://console.aws.amazon.com/organizations/. You must sign in as an IAM user, assume an IAM role, or sign in as the root user (not recommended) in the organization's master account.

2. On the **Accounts** tab, choose **Add account**.

3. Choose **Create account**.

4. Type the name that you want to assign to the account. This name helps you distinguish the account from all other accounts in the organization and is separate from the IAM alias or the email name of the owner.

5. Type the email address for the owner of the new account. This address must be unique to this account because it can be used to sign in as the root user of the account.

6. (Optional) Specify the name to assign to the IAM role that is automatically created in the new account. This role grants the organization's master account permission to access the newly created member account. If you don't specify a name, AWS Organizations gives the role a default name of `OrganizationAccountAccessRole`. **Important**
Remember this role name. You need it later to grant access to the new account for IAM users in the master account.

7. Choose **Create. Important**
If you get an error that indicates that you exceeded your account limits for the organization, contact AWS Customer Support. If you get an error that indicates that you can't add an account because your

organization is still initializing, wait one hour and try again. If the error persists, contact AWS Customer Support.

8. You are redirected to the **Accounts/All accounts** tab, showing your new account at the top of the list with its status set to **Pending creation**. This status changes to **Active** when the account is created. **Note**
By default, the **Accounts** tab hides account creation requests that failed. To show them, choose the switch at the top of the list and change it to **Show**.

9. Now that the account exists and has an IAM role that grants administrator access to users in the master account, you can access the account by following the steps in Accessing and Administering the Member Accounts in Your Organization.

When you create an account, AWS Organizations initially assigns a password to the root user that is a minimum of 64 characters long. All characters are randomly generated with no guarantees on the appearance of certain character sets. You can't retrieve this initial password. To access the account as the root user for the first time, you must go through the process for password recovery. For more information, see Accessing a Member Account as the Root User.

To create an AWS account that automatically is part of your organization (AWS CLI, AWS API)
You can use one of the following commands to create an account:

- AWS CLI: aws organizations create-account
- AWS API: CreateAccount

Accessing and Administering the Member Accounts in Your Organization

When you create an account in your organization, AWS Organizations automatically creates a root user and an IAM role for the account. However, AWS Organizations doesn't create any IAM users, groups, or other roles. To access the accounts in your organization, you must use one of the following methods:

- The account has a root user that you can use to sign in. We recommend that you use the root user only to create IAM users, groups, and roles, and then always sign in with one of those. See Accessing a Member Account as the Root User.
- If you create an account in your organization, you can access the account by using the preconfigured role that exists in all new accounts that are created this way. See Accessing a Member Account That Has a Master Account Access Role.
- If you invite an existing account to join your organization, and the account accepts the invitation, you can then create an IAM role that allows the master account to access the invited account, similar to the role automatically added to an account that is created with AWS Organizations. To create this role, see Creating the OrganizationAccountAccessRole in an Invited Member Account. After you create the role, you can access it using the steps in Accessing a Member Account That Has a Master Account Access Role.

Minimum permissions
To access an AWS account from any other account in your organization, you must have the following permission:
`sts:AssumeRole` – The `Resource` element must be set to either an asterisk (*) or the account ID number of the account with the user who needs to access the new member account

Accessing a Member Account as the Root User

When you create a new account, AWS Organizations initially assigns a password to the root user that is a minimum of 64 characters long. All characters are randomly generated with no guarantees on the appearance of certain character sets. You can't retrieve this initial password. To access the account as the root user for the first time, you must go through the process for password recovery.

Notes
As a best practice, we recommend that you don't use the root user to access your account except to create other users and roles with more limited permissions. Then sign in as one of those users or roles. We also recommend that you set multi-factor authentication (MFA) on the root user. Reset the password, and then assign an MFA device to the root user.

To request a new password for the root user of the member account (console)

1. Go to the sign-in page of the AWS console at https://console.aws.amazon.com/. If you are already signed in to AWS, you have to sign out to see the sign-in page.

2. If the **Sign in** page shows three text boxes for **Account ID or alias**, **IAM user name**, and **Password**, choose **Sign in using root account credentials**.

3. Type the email address that is associated with your AWS account, and then choose **Next**.

4. Choose **Forgot your password?**, and then type the information that is required to reset the password to a new one that you provide. To do this, you must be able to access incoming mail sent to the email address that is associated with the account.

Creating the OrganizationAccountAccessRole in an Invited Member Account

By default, if you create a member account as part of your organization, AWS automatically creates a role in the account that grants administrator permissions to delegated IAM users in the master account. By default, that role is named `OrganizationAccountAccessRole`. For more information, see Accessing a Member Account That Has a Master Account Access Role.

However, member accounts that you *invite* to join your organization ***do not*** automatically get an administrator role created. You have to do this manually, as shown in the following procedure. This essentially duplicates the role automatically set up for created accounts. We recommend that you use the same name, `OrganizationAccountAccessRole`, for your manually created roles for consistency and ease of remembering.

To create an AWS Organizations administrator role in a member account (console)

1. Sign in to the AWS Identity and Access Management (IAM) console at https://console.aws.amazon.com/iam/. You must sign in as an IAM user, assume an IAM role, or sign in as the root user (not recommended) in the member account that has permissions to create IAM roles and policies.

2. In the IAM console, navigate to **Roles**, and then choose **Create Role**.

3. Choose **Another AWS account**.

4. Type the 12-digit account ID number of the master account that you want to grant administrator access to.

5. For this role, because the accounts are internal to your company, you should not choose **Require external ID**. For more information about the external ID option, see When Should I Use the External ID? in the *IAM User Guide*.

6. If you have MFA enabled and configured, you can optionally choose to require authentication using an MFA device. For more information about MFA, see Using Multi-Factor Authentication (MFA) in AWS in the *IAM User Guide*.

7. On the **Attach permissions policies** page, choose the AWS managed policy named `AdministratorAccess`, and then choose **Next: Review**.

8. On the **Review** page, specify a role name and an optional description. We recommend that you use `OrganizationAccountAccessRole`, which is the default name assigned to the role in new accounts. To commit your changes, choose **Create role**.

9. Your new role appears on the list of available roles. Choose the new role's name to view the details, paying special note to the link URL that is provided. Give this URL to users in the member account who need to access the role. Also make note of the **Role ARN** because you need this in step 11.

10. Sign in to the IAM console at https://console.aws.amazon.com/iam/. This time, sign in as a user in the master account who has permissions to create policies and assign the policies to users or groups.

11. Navigate to **Policies**, and then choose **Create Policy. Note**
This example shows how to create a policy and attach it to a group. If you already created this policy for other accounts, you can skip to step 19.

12. For **Service**, choose **STS**.

13. For **Actions**, start typing **AssumeRole** in the **Filter** box, and then select the check box next to it when it appears.

14. Choose **Resources**, ensure that **Specific** is selected, and then choose **Add ARN**.

15. Type your AWS account ID number, and then type the name of the role that you previously created in steps 1–9.

16. If you are granting permission to assume the role in multiple member accounts, repeats steps 14 and 15 for each account.

17. Choose **Review policy**.

18. Type a name for the new policy, and then choose **Create policy** to save your changes.

19. Choose **Groups** in the navigation pane, and then choose the name of the group (not the check box) that you want to use to delegate administration of the member account.

20. Choose **Attach Policy**, select the policy that you created in steps 11–18, and then choose **Attach Policy**.

The users who are members of the selected group now can use the URLs that you captured in step 9 to access each member account's role. They can access these member accounts the same way as they would if accessing an account that you create in the organization. For more information about using the role to administer a member account, see Accessing a Member Account That Has a Master Account Access Role.

Accessing a Member Account That Has a Master Account Access Role

When you create a member account using the AWS Organizations console, AWS Organizations *automatically* creates an IAM role in the account. This role has full administrative permissions in the member account. The role is also configured to grant that access to the organization's master account. You can create an identical role for an invited member account by following the steps in Creating the OrganizationAccountAccessRole in an Invited Member Account. To use this role to access the member account, you must sign in as a user from the master account that has permissions to assume the role. To configure these permissions, perform the following procedure. We recommend that you grant permissions to groups instead of users for ease of maintenance.

To grant permissions to members of an IAM group in the master account to access the role (console)

1. Sign in to the IAM console at https://console.aws.amazon.com/iam/ as a user with administrator permissions in the master account. This is required to delegate permissions to the IAM group whose users will access the role in the member account.

2. In the navigation pane, choose **Groups** and then choose the name of the group (not the check box) whose members you want to be able to assume the role in the member account. If required, you can create a new group.

3. Choose the **Permissions** tab, and then expand the **Inline Policies** section.

4. If no inline policies exist, choose **click here** to create one. Otherwise, choose **Create Group Policy**.

5. Next to **Policy Generator**, choose **Select**.

6. On the **Edit Permissions** page, set the following options:

   - For **Effect**, choose **Allow**.

   - For **AWS Service**, choose **AWS Security Token Service**.

   - For **Actions**, choose **AssumeRole**.

   - For **Amazon Resource Name (ARN)**, type the ARN of the role that was created in the account. You can see the ARN in the IAM console on the role's **Summary** page. To construct this ARN, use the following template:

     ```
     arn:aws:iam::accountIdNumber:role/rolename
     ```

     Substitute the account ID number of the member account and the role name that was configured when you created the account. If you did not specify a role name, then the name defaults to `OrganizationAccountAccessRole`. The ARN should look like the following:

     ```
     arn:aws:iam::123456789012:role/OrganizationAccountAccessRole
     ```

7. Choose **Add statement**, and then choose **Next step**.

8. On the **Review Policy** page, ensure that the ARN for the role is correct. Type a name for the new policy, and then choose **Apply Policy**.

   IAM users that are members of the group now have permissions to switch to the new role in the AWS Management Console. When using the role, the user has administrator permissions in the new member account.

9. Provide the information to the user who will switch to the role in the console. The user needs the account number and the role name to enter manually in the AWS Management Console, or you can send the user a link that is constructed as shown in the following example. It is shown on multiple lines here for readability, but you should type it and provide it all as one line:

```
1 https://signin.aws.amazon.com/switchrole
2                 ?account=accountIdNumber
3                 &roleName=roleName
4                 &displayName=textToDisplay
```

The *textToDisplay* is a string that is displayed on the navigation bar in place of the user name.

For more information about granting permissions to switch roles, see Granting a User Permissions to Switch Roles in the *IAM User Guide*.

To manually switch to the role for the member account (console)

If you provide your users with a link formatted as shown in the preceding procedure, they simply have to click the link. They don't have to follow this procedure.

1. Sign in to the AWS Management Console as the master account user who was granted permissions in the preceding procedure. For example, you can use the IAM console at https://console.aws.amazon.com/iam/.

2. In the upper-right corner, choose the link that contains your current sign-in name and then choose **Switch role**.

3. Type the account ID number and role name that your administrator provided.

4. For **Display Name**, type the text that you want to show on the navigation bar in the upper-right corner in place of your user name while you are using the role. You can optionally choose a color.

5. Choose **Switch Role**. Now, all actions that you perform are done with the permissions granted to the role that you switched to. You no longer have the permissions associated with your original IAM user until you switch back.

6. When you are done performing actions that require the permissions of the role, you can switch back to your normal IAM user by choosing the role name in the upper-right corner (whatever you specified as the **Display Name**), and then choosing **Back to *UserName***.

For more information about using a role that you have been granted permissions to assume, see Switching to a Role (AWS Management Console) in the *IAM User Guide*.

For an end-to-end tutorial about using roles for cross-account access, see Tutorial: Delegate Access Across AWS Accounts Using IAM Roles in the *IAM User Guide*.

Removing a Member Account from Your Organization

An organization is a collection of AWS accounts that you centrally manage. In addition to creating accounts and managing invitations, you can perform the following tasks:

- Removing a Member Account from Your Organization
- Leaving an Organization as a Member Account
- Remove the Master Account and Delete the Organization

Important

You can remove an account from your organization only if the account has the information that is required for it to operate as a standalone account. When you create an account in an organization using the AWS Organizations console, API, or AWS CLI commands, all the information that is required of standalone accounts is not automatically collected. For each account that you want to make standalone, you must accept the AWS Customer Agreement, choose a support plan, provide and verify the required contact information, and provide a current payment method. AWS uses the payment method to charge for any billable (not AWS Free Tier) AWS activity that occurs while the account isn't attached to an organization.

Notes

Even after the removal of created accounts (accounts created using the AWS Organizations console or the `CreateAccount` API) from within an organization, (i) created accounts are governed by the terms of the creating master account's agreement with us, and (ii) the creating master account remains jointly and severally liable for any actions taken by its created accounts. Customers' agreements with us, and the rights and obligations under those agreements, cannot be assigned or transferred without our prior consent. To obtain our consent, contact us at https://aws.amazon.com/contact-us/. When a member account leaves an organization, that account no longer has access to cost and usage data from the time range when the account was a member of the organization. However, the master account of the organization can still access the data. If the account rejoins the organization, the account can access that data again.

Effects of Removing an Account from an Organization

When you remove an account from an organization, no direct changes are made to the account. However, the following indirect effects occur:

- The account is now responsible for paying its own charges and must have a valid payment method attached to the account.
- The principals in the account are no longer affected by any service control policies (SCPs) that were defined in the organization. This means that restrictions imposed by those SCPs are gone, and the users and roles in the account might have more permissions than they had before.
- Integration with other services might be disabled. For example, AWS Single Sign-On requires an organization to operate, so if you remove an account from an organization that supports AWS SSO, the users in that account can no longer use that service.

Removing a Member Account from Your Organization

When you sign in to the organization's master account, you can remove member accounts from the organization that you no longer need. To do this, complete the following procedure. These procedures apply only to member accounts. To remove the master account, you must delete the organization.

Note

If a member account is removed from an organization, that member account will no longer be covered by organization agreements. Master account administrators should communicate this to member accounts before removing member accounts from the organization, so that member accounts can put new agreements in place if necessary. A list of active organization agreements can be viewed in AWS Artifact Organization Agreements.

Minimum permissions

To remove one or more member accounts from your organization, you must sign in as an IAM user or role in the master account with the following permissions:

`organizations:DescribeOrganization` (console only) `organizations:RemoveAccountFromOrganization` If you choose to sign in as an IAM user or role in a member account in step 6, then that user or role must have the following permissions:

`organizations:DescribeOrganization` (console only). `organizations:LeaveOrganization` – Note that the organization administrator can apply a policy to your account that removes this permission, preventing you from removing your account from the organization. If you sign in as an IAM user and the account is missing payment information, the IAM user must have the permissions `aws-portal:ModifyBilling` and `aws-portal:ModifyPaymentMethods`. Also, the member account must have IAM user access to billing enabled. If this isn't already enabled, see Activating Access to the Billing and Cost Management Console in the *AWS Billing and Cost Management User Guide.*

To remove a member account from your organization (console)

1. Sign in to the Organizations console at https://console.aws.amazon.com/organizations/. You must sign in to the organization's master account.

2. On the **Accounts** tab, select the check box next to the member account that you want to remove from your organization. You can choose more than one.

3. Choose **Remove account**.

4. In the **Remove account** dialog box, choose **Remove**.

   A dialog box displays the success or failure status for each account.

5. If AWS Organizations fails to remove one or more of the accounts, it's typically because you have not provided all the required information for the account to operate as a standalone account. Perform the following steps:

   1. Choose **Sign in options** for one of the failed accounts.

   2. We recommend that you sign in to the member account by choosing **Copy link**, and then pasting it into the address bar of a new incognito browser window. If you don't use an incognito window, you're signed out of the master account and won't be able to navigate back to this dialog box.

   3. The browser takes you directly to the sign-up process to complete any steps that are missing for this account. Complete all the steps presented. They might include the following:

      - Provide contact information
      - Accept the AWS Customer Agreement
      - Provide a valid payment method
      - Verify the phone number
      - Select a support plan option

   4. After you complete the last sign-up step, AWS automatically redirects your browser to the AWS Organizations console for the member account. Choose **Leave organization**, and then confirm your choice in the confirmation dialog box. You are redirected to the **Getting Started** page of the AWS Organizations console, where you can view any pending invitations for your account to join other organizations.

To remove a member account from your organization (AWS CLI, AWS API)

You can use one of the following commands to remove a member account:

- AWS CLI: aws organizations remove-account-from-organization
- AWS API: RemoveAccountFromOrganization

Leaving an Organization as a Member Account

When signed in to a member account, you can remove that one account from its organization. To do this, complete the following procedure. The master account can't leave the organization using this technique. To remove the master account, you must delete the organization.

Note
If you leave an organization, you will no longer be covered by organization agreements that were accepted on your behalf by the master account of the organization. You can view a list of these organization agreements in AWS Artifact Organization Agreements. Before leaving the organization, you should determine (with the assistance of your legal, privacy, or compliance teams where appropriate) whether it is necessary for you to have new agreement(s) in place.

Minimum permissions
To leave an AWS organization, you must have the following permissions:
`organizations:DescribeOrganization` (console only). `organizations:LeaveOrganization` – Note that the organization administrator can apply a policy to your account that removes this permission, preventing you from removing your account from the organization. If you sign in as an IAM user and the account is missing payment information, the IAM user must have the permissions `aws-portal:ModifyBilling` and `aws-portal:ModifyPaymentMethods`. Also, the member account must have IAM user access to billing enabled. If this isn't already enabled, see Activating Access to the Billing and Cost Management Console in the *AWS Billing and Cost Management User Guide*.

Note
An account's status with an organization affects what cost and usage data is visible:
When a standalone account joins an organization, the account no longer has access to cost and usage data from the time range when the account was a standalone account. If a member account leaves an organization and becomes a standalone account, the account no longer has access to cost and usage data from the time range when the account was a member of the organization. The account has access only to the data that is generated as a standalone account. If a member account leaves organization A to join organization B, the account no longer has access to cost and usage data from the time range when the account was a member of organization A. The account has access only to the data that is generated as a member of organization B. If an account rejoins an organization that it previously belonged to, the account regains access to its historical cost and usage data.

To leave an organization as a member account (console)

1. Sign in to the Organizations console at https://console.aws.amazon.com/organizations/. You can sign in as an IAM user with the required permissions, or as the root user of the member account that you want to remove from the organization. By default, you don't have access to the root user password in a member account that was created using AWS Organizations. If required, recover the root user password by following the steps at Accessing a Member Account as the Root User.

2. On the **Organization overview** page, choose **Leave organization**.

3. Perform one of the following steps:

   - If your account has all the required information to operate as a standalone account, a confirmation dialog box appears. Confirm your choice to remove the account. You are redirected to the **Getting Started** page of the AWS Organizations console, where you can view any pending invitations for your account to join other organizations.

   - If your account doesn't have all the required information, perform the following steps:

     1. A dialog box appears to explain that you must complete some additional steps. Click the link.

     2. Complete all the sign-up steps that are presented. They might include the following:
        - Provide contact information
        - Accept the AWS Customer Agreement
        - Provide a valid payment method

- Verify the phone number
- Select a support plan option

3. When you see the dialog box stating that the sign-up process is complete, choose **Leave organization**.

4. A confirmation dialog box appears. Confirm your choice to remove the account. You are redirected to the **Getting Started** page of the AWS Organizations console, where you can view any pending invitations for your account to join other organizations.

To leave an organization as a member account (AWS CLI, AWS API)

You can use one of the following commands to leave an organization:

- AWS CLI: aws organizations leave-organization
- AWS API: LeaveOrganization

Closing an AWS Account

If you no longer need an AWS account (whether a member in an organization or not) and want to ensure that no one can accrue charges for it, you can close the account.

Before closing your account, back up any applications and data that you want to retain. All resources and data that were stored in the account are lost and cannot be recovered. For more information, see the KB article "How do I close my Amazon Web Services account?"

Immediately, the account can no longer be used for any AWS activity other than signing in as the root user to view past bills or to contact AWS Customer Support. For more information, see Contacting Customer Support About Your Bill.

Important
Accounts that are closed for a period of time are subject to permanent deletion after which the account and its resources can't be recovered. If you choose to close a member account without first removing it from the organization, the closed account still counts toward your limit on the number of accounts you can have in the organization. It's removed from your organization only after the account is permanently deleted. Instead of waiting, you can remove the account from the organization before closing it to avoid it counting against the limit.

You can close an account only by using the Billing and Cost Management console, not by using the AWS Organizations console or its tools.

- To close a member account, we recommend that you first remove the account from the organization and then close it using the steps in the following procedure.
- To close a master account, first remove the master account and delete the organization, and then close it using the steps in the following procedure.

To close an AWS account (console)

***Recommended: ***Before closing your account, back up any applications and data that you want to retain. AWS can't recover or restore your account resources and data after your account is closed.

1. Sign in as the root user of the account that you want to close, using the email address and password that are associated with the account. If you sign in as an IAM user or role, you can't close an account. **Note** By default, member accounts that you create with AWS Organizations don't have a password that's associated with the account's root user. To sign in, you must request a password for the root user. For more information, see Accessing a Member Account as the Root User.

2. Open the Billing and Cost Management console at https://console.aws.amazon.com/billing/home#/.

3. On the navigation bar in the upper-right corner, choose your account name (or alias) and then choose **My Account**.

4. On the **Account Settings** page, scroll to the end of the page to the **Close Account** section. Read and ensure that you understand the text next to the check box.

5. Select the check box to confirm your understanding of the terms, and then choose **Close Account**.

6. In the confirmation box, choose **Close Account**.

After you close an AWS account, you can no longer use it to access AWS services or resources. You can only view the account's past bills and access AWS Customer Support. You can reopen the account by contacting AWS Support. For more information, see How do I reopen my closed AWS account? in the Knowledge Center.

Managing Organizational Units (OUs)

You can use organizational units (OUs) to group accounts together to administer as a single unit. This greatly simplifies the management of your accounts. For example, you can attach a policy-based control to an OU, and all accounts within the OU automatically inherit the policy. You can create multiple OUs within a single organization, and you can create OUs within other OUs. Each OU can contain multiple accounts, and you can move accounts from one OU to another. However, OUs must be unique within a root (no duplications of names).

Note
Currently, you can have only a single root, which AWS Organizations creates for you when you first set up your organization. The name of the default root is "root."

To structure the accounts in your organization, you can perform the following tasks:

- Viewing details of an OU
- Creating an OU
- Renaming an OU
- Moving an account to an OU or between the root and OUs

Navigating the Root and OU Hierarchy

To navigate to different OUs or to the root when moving accounts or attaching policies, you can use the tree view.

To enable and use the tree view of the organization

1. Sign in to the Organizations console at https://console.aws.amazon.com/organizations/.

2. Choose the **Organize accounts** tab.

3. If the tree view pane isn't visible on the left side of the page, choose the **TREE VIEW** switch icon 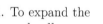.

4. The tree initially appears showing the root, with only the first level of child OUs displayed. To expand the tree to show deeper levels, choose the + icon next to any parent entity. To reduce clutter and collapse a branch of the tree, choose the — icon next to an expanded parent entity.

5. Choose the OU or root that you want to navigate to. The node in the tree view that is displayed in bold text is the one that you are currently viewing in the center pane.

Notes
Rename, Delete, and Move operations in the center pane: When you view the contents of a root or OU in the console, you can interact with the child entities of that root or OU. For example, if you select the check box for a child OU or account, you can choose the **Rename**, **Delete**, or **Move** links above that section to perform those operations on the selected entity. The operations apply *only* to the child entities that you select. They don't apply to the containing root or OU. To perform the same operations for the containing OU, you must navigate to the OU's parent OU or root, and then select the check box for the child OU that you want to manage. **Details pane**: The details pane on the right side of the console shows information about the root or OU that you are viewing. If you select a check box for a child entity, the details pane switches to show information about the selected entity. To see the details of the containing root or OU again, you must clear the check box. Alternatively, you can navigate to the parent root or OU, and then select the check box for the OU whose information you want to see.

To navigate without using the tree view

1. Sign in to the Organizations console at https://console.aws.amazon.com/organizations/.

2. Choose the **Organize accounts** tab.

3. Navigate down a branch by choosing the name of the OU (not the check box) that you want to view in the center pane.

4. Navigate up the branch by choosing the back button (<) on the title bar of the center pane.

Creating an OU

When signed in to your organization's master account, you can create an OU in your organization's root. OUs can be nested up to five levels deep. To create an OU, complete the following steps.

Minimum permissions
To create an OU within a root in your organization, you must have the following permissions:
`organizations:DescribeOrganization` (console only) `organizations:CreateOrganizationalUnit`

To create an OU (Console)

1. Sign in to the Organizations console at https://console.aws.amazon.com/organizations/. You must sign in as an IAM user, assume an IAM role, or sign in as the root user (not recommended) in the organization's master account.

   The console displays the contents of the root. The first time you visit a root, the console displays all of your AWS accounts in that top-level view. If you previously created OUs and moved accounts into them, the console shows only the top-level OUs and any accounts that you have not yet moved into an OU.

2. (Optional) If you want to create an OU inside an existing OU, navigate to the child OU by choosing the name (not the check box) of the child OU, or by choosing the OU in the tree view.

3. When you're in the correct location in the hierarchy, choose **Create organizational unit (OU)**.

4. In the **Create organizational unit** dialog box, type the name of the OU that you want to create, and then choose **Create organizational unit**.

   Your new OU appears inside the parent. You now can move accounts to this OU or attach policies to it.

To create an OU (AWS CLI, AWS API)
You can use one of the following commands to create an OU:

- AWS CLI: aws organizations create-organizational-unit
- AWS API: CreateOrganizationalUnit

Renaming an OU

When signed in to your organization's master account, you can rename an OU. To do this, complete the following steps.

Minimum permissions
To rename an OU within a root in your AWS organization, you must have the following permissions:
`organizations:DescribeOrganization` (console only) `organizations:UpdateOrganizationalUnit`

To rename an OU (Console)

1. Sign in to the Organizations console at https://console.aws.amazon.com/organizations/. You must sign in as an IAM user, assume an IAM role, or sign in as the root user (not recommended) in the organization's master account.

2. On the **Organize accounts** tab, navigate to the parent of the OU that you want to rename. Select the check box for the child OU that you want to rename.

3. Choose **Rename** above the list of OUs.

4. In the **Rename organizational unit** dialog box, type a new name, and then choose **Rename organizational unit**.

To rename an OU (AWS CLI, AWS API)

You can use one of the following commands to rename an OU:

- AWS CLI: aws organizations update-organizational-unit
- AWS API: UpdateOrganizationalUnit

Moving an Account to an OU or Between the Root and OUs

When signed in to your organization's master account, you can move accounts in your organization from the root to an OU, from one OU to another, or back to the root from an OU. Placing an account inside an OU makes it subject to any policies that are attached to the parent OU and any other OUs in the parent chain up to the root. If an account isn't in an OU, it's subject to only the policies that are attached to the root and any that are attached directly to the account. To move an account, complete the following steps.

Minimum permissions

To move an account to a new location in the OU hierarchy, you must have the following permissions:
`organizations:DescribeOrganization` (console only) `organizations:MoveAccount`

To move an account to an OU (console)

1. Sign in to the Organizations console at https://console.aws.amazon.com/organizations/. You must sign in as an IAM user, assume an IAM role, or sign in as the root user (not recommended) in the organization's master account.

2. Choose the **Organize accounts** tab and then navigate to the OU that contains the account that you want to move. When you find the account, select its check box. Select multiple check boxes if you want to move multiple accounts.

3. Choose **Move ** above the list of accounts.

4. In the **Move accounts** dialog box, choose the OU or the root that you want to move the accounts to and then choose **Select**.

To move an account to an OU (AWS CLI, AWS API)

You can use one of the following commands to move an account:

- AWS CLI: aws organizations move-account
- AWS API: MoveAccount

Deleting an OU That You No Longer Need

When signed in to your organization's master account, you can delete OUs that you no longer need. You first must move all accounts out of the OU and any child OUs, and then delete the child OUs.

Minimum permissions

To delete an OU, you must have the following permissions:
`organizations:DescribeOrganization` (console only) `organizations:DeleteOrganizationalUnit`

To delete an OU (Console)

1. Sign in to the Organizations console at https://console.aws.amazon.com/organizations/. You must sign in as an IAM user, assume an IAM role, or sign in as the root user (not recommended) in the organization's master account.

2. On the **Organize accounts** tab, navigate to the parent container of the OU that you want to delete. Select the OU's check box. You can select check boxes for multiple OUs if you want to delete more than one.

3. Choose **Delete** above the list of OUs.

    AWS Organizations deletes the OU and removes it from the list.

To delete an OU (AWS CLI, AWS API)
You can use one of the following commands to delete an OU:

- AWS CLI: aws organizations delete-organizational-unit
- AWS API: DeleteOrganizationalUnit

Managing Organization Policies

Policies in AWS Organizations enable you to apply additional types of management to the AWS accounts in your organization. Policies are enabled only after you enable all features in your organization. You can apply policies to the following entities in your organization:

- **A root** – A policy applied to a root applies to all accounts in the organization
- **An OU** – A policy applied to an OU applies to all accounts in the OU and to any child OUs
- **An account** – A policy applied to an account applies only to that one account

Notes

Service control policies never apply to the master account, no matter which root or OU the master account is located in. Currently, service control policy (SCP) is the only supported policy type. Policy types are *available* to use in an organization when you enable all features. However, at the root level, you can disable an individual policy type using the EnablePolicyType and DisablePolicyType operations. Use the DescribeOrganization API operation to determine what organization policy types are available to use. Use the `ListRoots` API operation to see which policy types are enabled and disabled in each root.

The AWS Organizations console can also display the enabled and disabled policy types. On the **Organize accounts** tab, choose the `Root` in the navigation pane on the left. The details pane on the right shows all of the available policy types and indicates which are enabled and which are disabled.

For procedures that are specific to each type of policy, see the following topics:

- **Service control policies**. Service control policies (SCPs) are similar to IAM permission policies and use almost the exact same syntax. However, an SCP never grants permissions. Instead, think of an SCP as a "filter" that enables you to restrict what service and actions can be accessed by users and roles in the accounts that you attach the SCP to. An SCP applied at the root cascades its permissions to the OUs below it. An OU at the next level down gets the mathematical intersection of the permissions flowing down from the parent root and the SCPs that are attached to the child OU. In other words, any account has only those permissions permitted by *every* OU and the parent root above it. If a permission is blocked at any level above the account, either implicitly (by not being included in an "Allow" policy statement) or explicitly (by being included in a "Deny" policy statement), a user or role in the affected account can't use that permission, even if the account administrator attaches the `AdministratorAccess` IAM policy with */* permissions to the user.

Important

When you disable a policy type in a root, all policies of that type are automatically detached from all entities in that root. If you reenable the policy type, that root reverts to the default state for that policy type. For example, if you reenable SCPs in a root, all entities in that root are initially attached only to the default SCP `FullAWSAccess` policy. Any attachments of policies to entities from before the policy type was disabled are lost and aren't automatically recoverable.

The following procedures apply to *all* policy types. You must enable a policy type in a root before you can attach policies of that type to any entities in that root.

Topics

- Listing and Displaying Information about Organization Policies
- Editing a Policy
- Enabling and Disabling a Policy Type on a Root
- Attaching a Policy to Roots, OUs, or Accounts
- Detaching a Policy from Roots, OUs, or Accounts
- Deleting a Policy
- Service Control Policies

Listing and Displaying Information about Organization Policies

This section describes various ways to get details about the policies in your organization.

Listing All Policies in the Organization

Minimum permissions
To list the policies within your organization, you must have the following permission:
`organizations:ListPolicies`

To list all policies in the organization (Console)

1. Sign in to the Organizations console at https://console.aws.amazon.com/organizations/. You must sign in as an IAM user, assume an IAM role, or sign in as the root user (not recommended) in the organization's master account.

2. Choose the **Policies** tab.

   The displayed list includes the policies of all types that are currently defined in the organization.

To list all policies in an organization (AWS CLI, AWS API)
You can use one of the following commands to list policies in an organization:

- AWS CLI: aws organizations list-policies
- AWS API: ListPolicies

Listing All Policies Attached to a Root, OU, or Account

Minimum permissions
To list the policies that are attached to a root, OU, or account within your organization, you must have the following permission:
`organizations:ListPoliciesForTarget` with a `Resource` element in the same policy statement that includes the ARN of the specified target (or "*")

To list all policies that are attached directly to a specified root, OU, or account (console)

1. Sign in to the Organizations console at https://console.aws.amazon.com/organizations/. You must sign in as an IAM user, assume an IAM role, or sign in as the root user (not recommended) in the organization's master account.

2. On the **Organize accounts** tab, navigate to the root, OU, or account whose policy attachments you want to see.

   1. For a root or OU, do not select any check boxes. This way, the details pane on the right shows the information about the root or OU that you are viewing. Alternatively, you can navigate to the parent of the OU, and then select the check box for the OU whose information you want to see.

   2. For an account, check the box for the account.

3. In the details pane on the right, expand the **Service control policies** section.

   The displayed list shows all policies that are attached directly to this entity. It also shows policies that affect this entity because of inheritance from the root or a parent OU.

To list all policies that are attached directly to a specified root, OU, or account (AWS CLI, AWS API)
You can use one of the following commands to list policies that are attached to an entity:

- AWS CLI: aws organizations list-policies-for-target
- AWS API: ListPoliciesForTarget

Listing All Roots, OUs, and Accounts That a Policy Is Attached To

Minimum permissions

To list the entities that a policy is attached to, you must have the following permission:
`organizations:ListTargetsForPolicy` with a `Resource` element in the same policy statement that includes the ARN of the specified policy (or "*")

To list all roots, OUs, and accounts that have a specified policy attached (console)

1. Choose the **Policies** tab, and select the check box next to the policy that you're interested in.

2. In the details pane on the right, choose one of the following:

   - **Accounts** to see the list of accounts that the policy is directly attached to
   - **Organizational units** to see the list of OUs that the policy is directly attached to
   - **Roots** to see the list of roots that the policy is directly attached to

To list all roots, OUs, and accounts that have a specified policy attached (AWS CLI, AWS API)

You can use one of the following commands to list entities that have a policy:

   - AWS CLI: aws organizations list-targets-for-policy
   - AWS API: ListTargetsForPolicy

Getting Details About a Policy

Minimum permissions

To display the details of a policy, you must have the following permission:
`organizations:DescribePolicy` with a `Resource` element in the same policy statement that includes the ARN of the specified policy (or "*")

To get details about a policy (console)

1. Choose the **Policies** tab and select the check box next to the policy that you're interested in.

   The Details pane on the right displays the available information about the policy, including its ARN, description, and attachments.

2. To view the content of the policy, choose **Policy editor**.

   The center pane shows the following information:

   - The details about the policy: its name, description, unique ID, and ARN.

   - The list of roots, OUs, and accounts that the policy is attached to. Choose each item to see the individual entities of each type.

   - The policy's content (specific to the type of policy):

     - For SCPs, the JSON text that defines the permissions that are allowed in attached accounts

     To update the contents of the policy document, choose **Edit** . Choose **Save** when you are done. For more details, see the next section.

To get details about a policy (AWS CLI, AWS API)

You can use one of the following commands to get details about a policy:

   - AWS CLI: aws organizations describe-policy
   - AWS API: DescribePolicy

Editing a Policy

Minimum permissions
To display the details of a policy, you must have the following permissions:
`organizations:DescribePolicy` with a `Resource` element in the same policy statement that includes the ARN of the specified policy (or "*") `organizations:UpdatePolicy` with a `Resource` element in the same policy statement that includes the ARN of the specified policy (or "*")

Enabling and Disabling a Policy Type on a Root

Before you can attach a policy of any type to a root, you must first enable that root to support the specified type of policy.

Note
Currently, you can have only one root in an organization. Currently, the only supported policy type is SCP.

Important
When you disable a policy type in a root, all policies of that type are automatically detached from all entities in that root. If you reenable the policy type, that root reverts to the default state for that policy type. For example, if you reenable SCPs in a root, all entities in that root are initially attached to only the default `FullAWSAccess` policy. Any attachments of policies to entities from before the policy type was disabled are lost and aren't automatically recoverable.

Note
The AWS Organizations console can display the enabled and disabled status of each policy type. On the **Organize accounts** tab, choose the `Root` in the left navigation pane. The details pane on the right side of the screen shows all of the available policy types available and indicates which are enabled and which are disabled in that root. If the option to **Enable** a type is present, that type is currently disabled. If the option to **Disable** a type is present, that type is currently enabled.

Minimum permissions
To enable a policy type in a root in your organization, you must have the following permissions:
`organizations:EnablePolicyType organizations:DescribeOrganization`

To enable or disable a policy type on a root (console)

When you sign in to your organization's master account, you can enable or disable policy types on a root.

1. Sign in to the Organizations console at https://console.aws.amazon.com/organizations/. You must sign in as an IAM user, assume an IAM role, or sign in as the root user (not recommended) in the organization's master account.

2. On the **Organize accounts** tab, choose **Root** in the left navigation pane.

3. In the details pane on the right side of the screen, next to **Service control policies**, choose **Enable** or **Disable**. Note
You must first detach all policies of the specified type from all entities in a root before you can disable the policy type in that root.

To enable or disable a policy type on a root (AWS CLI, AWS API)
You can use one of the following commands to disable a policy type:

- AWS CLI: aws organizations enable-policy-type and aws organizations disable-policy-type
- AWS API: EnablePolicyType and DisablePolicyType

Attaching a Policy to Roots, OUs, or Accounts

When signed in to your organization's master account, you can attach a policy that you previously created to the root, to an OU, or directly to an account. To attach a policy, complete the following steps.

Minimum permissions
To attach a policy to a root, OU, or account, you must have the following permission:
`organizations:AttachPolicy` with a `Resource` element in the same policy statement that includes "*" or the ARN of the specified policy and the ARN of the root, OU, or account that you want to attach the policy to

To attach a policy to a root, OU, or account (console)

1. Sign in to the Organizations console at https://console.aws.amazon.com/organizations/. You must sign in as an IAM user, assume an IAM role, or sign in as the root user (not recommended) in the organization's master account.

2. On the **Organize accounts** tab, navigate to and select the check box for the root, OU, or account you want to attach the policy to.

3. In the **Details** pane on the right, expand the **CONTROL POLICIES** section to see the list of the currently attached policies, and then choose **Attach policy**.

4. On the list of available policies, find the one that you want and choose **Attach**. The list of attached policies is updated with the new addition. The policy goes into effect immediately. For example, an SCP immediately affects the permissions of IAM users and roles in the attached account or all accounts under the attached root or OU.

To attach a policy to a root, OU, or account (AWS CLI, AWS API)
You can use one of the following commands to attach a policy:

- AWS CLI: aws organizations attach-policy
- AWS API: AttachPolicy

Detaching a Policy from Roots, OUs, or Accounts

When signed in to your organization's master account, you can detach a policy from the root, OU, or account that it is attached to. After you detach a policy from an entity, that policy no longer applies to any account that was affected by the now detached entity. To detach a policy, complete the following steps.

Note
You can't detach the last SCP from an entity. There must be at least one SCP attached to all entities at all times.

Minimum permissions
To detach a policy from a root, OU, or account, you must have the following permission:
`organizations:DetachPolicy`

To detach a policy from a root, OU, or account (console)

1. Sign in to the Organizations console at https://console.aws.amazon.com/organizations/. You must sign in as an IAM user, assume an IAM role, or sign in as the root user (not recommended) in the organization's master account.

2. On the **Organize accounts** tab, navigate to and select the check box for the root, OU, or account from which you want to detach the policy.

3. In the **Details** pane on the right, expand the **CONTROL POLICIES** section to see the list of the currently attached policies. The **Source** field tells you where the policy comes from. It can be attached directly to the account or OU, or it could be attached to a parent OU or root.

4. Choose the **X** next to the policy that you want to detach. The list of attached policies is updated with the chosen policy removed. The policy change caused by detaching the policy goes into effect immediately. For example, detaching a SCP immediately affects the permissions of IAM users and roles in the formerly attached account or accounts under the formerly attached root or OU.

To detach a policy from a root, OU, or account (AWS CLI, AWS API)
You can use one of the following commands to detach a policy:

- AWS CLI: aws organizations detach-policy
- AWS API: DetachPolicy

Deleting a Policy

When signed in to your organization's master account, you can delete a policy that you no longer need in your organization.

Notes
Before you can delete a policy, you must first detach it from all attached entities. You cannot delete any AWS-managed SCP such as the one named `FullAWSAccess`.

To delete a policy, complete the following steps.

Minimum permissions
To delete a policy, you must have the following permission:
`organizations:DeletePolicy`

To delete a policy (console)

1. Sign in to the Organizations console at https://console.aws.amazon.com/organizations/. You must sign in as an IAM user, assume an IAM role, or sign in as the root user (not recommended) in the organization's master account.

2. The policy that you want to delete must first be detached from all roots, OUs, and accounts. Follow the steps in Detaching a Policy from Roots, OUs, or Accounts to detach the policy from all entities in the organization.

3. On the **Policies** tab, choose **All policies** and then select the policy that you want to delete.

4. Choose **Delete policy**.

5. In the **Delete policy** dialog box, choose **Delete**.

To delete a policy (AWS CLI, AWS API)
You can use one of the following commands to delete a policy:

- AWS CLI: aws organizations delete-policy
- AWS API: DeletePolicy

Service Control Policies

Service control policies (SCPs) are one type of policy that you can use to manage your organization. SCPs enable you to restrict, at the account level of granularity, what services and actions the users, groups, and roles in those accounts can do.

For additional details about SCPs, strategies for using them, and their syntax, see About Service Control Policies.

For example SCPs that you can copy and paste and customize for your use, see Example Service Control Policies.

SCPs are available only in an organization that has all features enabled. SCPs aren't available if your organization has enabled only the consolidated billing features.

SCPs are similar to IAM permission policies and use almost the exact same syntax. However, an SCP never grants permissions. Instead, think of an SCP as a filter that enables you to restrict what service and actions can be accessed by users and roles in the accounts that you attach the SCP to. An SCP that is applied at the root cascades its permissions to the OUs below it. An OU at the next level down gets the mathematical intersection of the permissions that flow down from the parent root and the SCPs that are attached to the OU. In other words, any account has only those permissions permitted by *every* parent above it. If a permission is blocked at any level above the account, either implicitly (by not being included in an `Allow` policy statement) or explicitly (by being included in a `Deny` policy statement), a user or role in the affected account cannot use that permission, even if the account administrator attaches the `AdministratorAccess` IAM policy with */* permissions to the user.

Warning
We strongly recommend that you don't attach SCPs to the root of your organization without thoroughly testing the impact that the policy has on accounts. Instead, create an OU that you can move your accounts into one at a time, or at least in small numbers, to ensure that you don't inadvertently lock users out of key services. One way to determine whether a service is used by an account is to examine the service last accessed data in IAM. Another way is to use AWS CloudTrail to log service usage at the API level.

Note
All characters that you type count against the size limit of your SCP. The examples in this guide show the SCPs formatted with extra white space to improve their readability. However, to save space if your policy size approaches the limit, you can delete any white space, such as space characters and line breaks that are outside quotation marks.

Considerations

- Users and roles must still be granted permissions with appropriate IAM permission policies. A user without any IAM permission policies has no access at all, even if the applicable SCPs allow all services and all actions.
- Remember that SCPs are filters that *limit* what access can be exercised in an account.
- SCPs don't grant permissions to any user or role.
- If a user or role has an IAM permission policy that grants access to an action that is also allowed by the applicable SCPs, the user or role can perform that action.
- If a user or role has an IAM permission policy that grants access to an action that is either not allowed or explicitly denied by the applicable SCPs, the user or role can't perform that action.

Important
SCPs affect all users and roles in attached accounts, ***including the root user***. The only exceptions are those described in the following list of tasks that aren't affected and can't be restricted by using SCPs. SCPs ***do not ***affect any service-linked role. Service-linked roles enable other AWS services to integrate with AWS Organizations and can't be restricted by SCPs. SCPs *affect only principals* that are managed by accounts that are part of the organization. They don't affect users or roles from accounts outside the organization. For example, consider an Amazon S3 bucket that's owned by account A in an organization. The bucket policy grants access to users from accounts outside the organization. Account A has an SCP attached. That SCP doesn't apply to those outside users. It applies only to users that are managed by account A in the organization. When

you disable the SCP policy type in a root, all SCPs are automatically detached from all entities in that root. If you reenable SCPs in a root, that root reverts to only the default `FullAWSAccess` policy automatically attached to all entities in the root. Any attachments of SCPs to entities from before SCPs were disabled are lost and raren't automatically recoverable, although you can manually reattach them.

Tasks and entities not restricted by SCPs

- Any action performed using permissions that are attached to a service-linked role.
- Managing root credentials. No matter what SCPs are attached, the root user in an account can always do the following:
  - Changing the root user's password
  - Creating, updating, or deleting root access keys
  - Enabling or disabling multi-factor authentication on the root user
  - Creating, updating, or deleting x.509 keys for the root user
- Registering for the Enterprise support plan as the root user
- Closing an account as the root user (from within the account instead of submitting a ticket to AWS Support)
- Changing the AWS support level as the root user
- Managing Amazon CloudFront keys
- Trusted signer functionality for CloudFront private content
- Modifying AWS account email allowance/rDNS
- Performing tasks on some AWS-related services:
  - Alexa Top Sites
  - Alexa Web Information Service
  - Amazon Mechanical Turk
  - Amazon Product Marketing API

You can use the procedures in the following sections to create and update SCPs.

To learn more about policy types, see Managing Organization Policies.

Creating a Service Control Policy

When signed in with permissions to your organization's master account, you can create an SCP. To create an SCP, complete the following steps.

Minimum permissions
To create a policy within your organization, you must have the following permission:
`organizations:CreatePolicy`

To create a service control policy (console)

1. Sign in to the Organizations console at https://console.aws.amazon.com/organizations/. You must sign in as an IAM user, assume an IAM role, or sign in as the root user (not recommended) in the organization's master account.

2. On the **Policies** tab, choose **Create Policy**.

3. Choose the technique that you want to use to create the policy:

   - **Policy generator** – Select services and actions from a list. The generator uses your choices to create an SCP for you.
   - **Copy an existing SCP** – Make a copy of an existing SCP and customize it to meet your new requirements, or create a new SCP using a policy text editor.

4. If you chose **Policy generator**, follow these steps:

   1. Type a name and a description for the SCP that will help you find it and remember its intended purpose later.

2. Choose an **Effect**. The effect applies only to this one policy statement. Each statement can have its own effect.

  - Specify **Deny** if you want to create a blacklist that blocks all access to the specified services and actions. This kind of policy is intended to be used in addition to a policy like `FullAWSAccess` that grants permissions. The explicit `Deny` on specific actions in the blacklist policy overrides the `Allow` in any other policy.
  - Specify **Allow** if you want to create a whitelist that specifies the services and actions to which users can be granted access. Remember that by default there's already a `FullAWSAccess` policy that grants all permissions attached to every root, OU, and account. So if you want to allow a more limited set of services and actions, you must replace the default policy with a new policy that allows fewer permissions.

3. In the **Statement builder**, select the service whose actions you want to allow or deny.

4. Also in the **Statement builder**, select the actions in that service that you want to specify in this policy. You can choose **Select All** or select multiple actions from the list.

5. Choose **Add statement** to add it to the current SCP under construction.

6. Repeat the preceding two steps as often as you need to add more statements to the SCP.

7. When your SCP includes all the statements that you need, choose **Create policy** to save the completed SCP.

5. If you instead chose **Copy an existing SCP**, follow these steps: **Note**
You can use this option to create a new SCP using the editor. Don't select a policy to copy—just fill in the name and type your desired policy text.

  1. Choose **Select a policy** and then choose the SCP that you want to copy to use as a starting point. You can type in the **Filter** box to narrow your choices if the list is long.

  2. For **Policy name** and **Description**, type a name and a description for the policy that will help you find it and remember its intended purpose later.

  3. In **Edit policy**, edit the copy of the SCP to meet your new requirements. If you didn't choose an SCP from the list, this box is empty, and you can type a new policy.

  4. When you are done, choose **Create** to save your completed SCP.

Your new SCP appears in the list of the organization's policies. You can now attach your SCP to the root, OUs, or accounts.

To create a service control policy (AWS CLI, AWS API)
You can use one of the following commands to create an SCP:

  - AWS CLI: aws organizations create-policy
  - AWS API: CreatePolicy

Updating a Service Control Policy

When signed in to your organization's master account, you can rename or change the contents of a policy. To do this, complete the following steps.

Note
Changing the contents of an SCP immediately affects any users, groups, and roles in all attached accounts.

Minimum permissions
To update a policy in your AWS organization, you must have the following permissions:
organizations:UpdatePolicy organizations:DescribeOrganization

To update a policy (console)

1. Sign in to the Organizations console at https://console.aws.amazon.com/organizations/. You must sign in as an IAM user, assume an IAM role, or sign in as the root user (not recommended) in the organization's master account.

2. Choose the **Policies** tab.

3. Choose the policy that you want to update.

4. In the details pane on the right, choose **Policy editor**.

   The editor window opens initially in read-only mode in the center pane.

5. Choose **Edit** to enable making changes to the policy.

6. Make your changes and then choose **Save**.

To update a policy (AWS CLI, AWS API)

You can use one of the following commands to update a policy:

- AWS CLI: aws organizations update-policy
- AWS API: UpdatePolicy

About Service Control Policies

A service control policy (SCP) determines what services and actions can be delegated by administrators to the users and roles in the accounts that the SCP is applied to. An SCP *does not* grant any permissions. Instead, think of it as a filter. If the SCP allows the actions for a service, the administrator of the account can grant permissions for those actions to the users and roles in that account, and the users and roles can perform the actions if the administrators grant those permissions. If the SCP denies actions for a service, the administrators in that account cannot effectively grant permissions for those actions, and the users and roles in the account can't perform the actions even if granted by an administrator. For example, you can specify that the administrators of account 111122223333 can grant permissions only to Amazon Simple Storage Service (Amazon S3) and Amazon Elastic Compute Cloud (Amazon EC2), and the administrators of account 777788889999 can grant permissions only to Amazon DynamoDB (DynamoDB).

Important

SCPs *do not* affect the master account no matter where the account is in the root/OU hierarchy. SCPs *do* affect the root user along with all IAM users and standard IAM roles in any affected account. SCPs *do not* affect any service-linked role in an account. These roles exist to support integration with other AWS services and can't be restricted by SCPs. SCPs *affect only principals* that are managed by accounts that are part of the organization. They don't affect users or roles from accounts outside the organization. For example, consider an Amazon S3 bucket that is owned by account A in an organization. The bucket policy grants access to users from accounts outside the organization. Account A has an SCP attached. That SCP doesn't apply to those outside users. It applies only to users that are managed by account "A" in the organization. SCPs are available only in organizations that enable all features. SCPs aren't available if your organization has enabled only the consolidated billing features.

The following illustration shows how SCPs work.

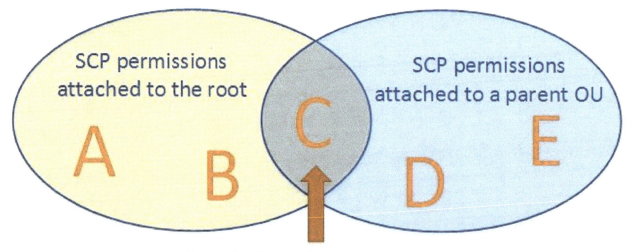

In this illustration, the root has an SCP attached that allows permissions A, B, and C. An OU in that root has an SCP that allows C, D, and E. Because the root's OU doesn't allow D or E, nothing in the root or any of its children can use them, including the parent OU. Even though the parent OU explicitly allows them, they end up blocked because they're blocked by the root. Also, because the OU's SCP doesn't allow A or B, those permissions are blocked for the parent OU and any of its children. However, other OUs under the root that are peers to the parent OU could allow A and B.

Users and roles must still be granted permissions using IAM permission policies attached to them or to groups. The SCPs filter the permissions granted by such policies, and the user can't perform any actions that the applicable SCPs don't allow. Actions allowed by the SCPs can be used if they are granted to the user or role by one or more IAM permission policies.

When you attach SCPs to the root, OUs, or directly to accounts, all policies that affect a given account are evaluated together using the same rules that govern IAM permission policies:

- Any action that has an explicit `Deny` in an SCP cannot be delegated to users or roles in the affected accounts. An explicit `Deny` statement overrides any `Allow` that other SCPs might grant.
- Any action that has an explicit `Allow` in an SCP (such as the default "*" SCP or by any other SCP that calls out a specific service or action) can be delegated to users and roles in the affected accounts.
- Any action that isn't explicitly allowed by an SCP is implicitly denied and can't be delegated to users or roles in the affected accounts.

By default, an SCP named `FullAWSAccess` is attached to every root, OU, and account. This default SCP allows all actions and all services. So in a new organization, until you start creating or manipulating the SCPs, all of your existing IAM permissions continue to operate as they did. As soon as you apply a new or modified SCP to a root or OU that contains an account, the permissions that your users have in that account become filtered by the SCP. Permissions that used to work might now be denied if they are not allowed by the SCP at every level of the hierarchy down to the specified account.

If you disable the SCP policy type in a root, all SCPs are automatically detached from all entities in that root. If you reenable SCPs in that root, all the original attachments are lost, and all entities are reset to being attached to only the default `FullAWSAccess` SCP.

For details about the syntax of SCPs, see Service Control Policy Syntax in the Reference section of this guide.

Strategies for Using SCPs

You can configure the SCPs in your organization to work as either of the following:

- A blacklist – actions are allowed by default, and you specify what services and actions are prohibited
- A whitelist – actions are prohibited by default, and you specify what services and actions are allowed

Using SCPs as a Blacklist

The default configuration of AWS Organizations supports using SCPs as blacklists. Account administrators can delegate all services and actions until you create and attach a policy that denies (blacklists) a specific service or set of actions.

To support this, AWS Organizations attaches an AWS-managed SCP named FullAWSAccess to every root and OU when it's created. This policy allows all services and actions. Because the policy is an AWS-managed SCP, it can't be modified or deleted. It's always available for you to attach or detach from the entities in your organization as needed. The policy looks like this:

```
1  {
2      "Version": "2012-10-17",
3      "Statement": [
4          {
5              "Effect": "Allow",
6              "Action": "*",
7              "Resource": "*"
8          }
9      ]
10 }
```

This enables account administrators to delegate permissions for any service or action until you create and attach an SCP that explicitly prohibits those actions that you don't want users and roles in certain accounts to perform.

Such a policy might look like the following example, which prevents users in the affected accounts from performing any actions for the DynamoDB service. The organization administrator can detach the `FullAWSAccess` policy and attach this one instead. Note that this SCP still allows all other services and their actions:

```
1  {
2      "Version": "2012-10-17",
3      "Statement": [
4          {
5              "Sid": "AllowsAllActions",
6              "Effect": "Allow",
7              "Action": "*",
8              "Resource": "*"
9          },
10         {
11             "Sid": "DenyDynamoDB",
12             "Effect": "Deny",
13             "Action": "dynamodb:*",
14             "Resource": "*"
15         }
16     ]
17 }
```

The users in the affected accounts cannot perform DynamoDB actions because the explicit `Deny` element in the second statement overrides the explicit `Allow` in the first. You could also configure this by leaving the `FullAWSAccess` policy in place and then attaching a second policy that has only the `Deny` statement in it, as shown here:

```
1  {
2      "Version": "2012-10-17",
3      "Statement": [
4          {
5              "Effect": "Deny",
6              "Action": "dynamodb:*",
7              "Resource": "*"
8          }
9      ]
10 }
```

The combination of the `FullAWSAccess` policy and the `Deny` statement in the preceding DynamoDB policy that is applied to a root or OU has the exact same effect as the single policy that contains both statements. All policies that apply at a specified level are combined together, and each statement, no matter which policy originated it, gets evaluated according to the rules discussed earlier (that is, an ***explicit*** Deny overrides an ***explicit ***Allow, which overrides the default ***implicit ***Deny).

Using SCPs as a Whitelist

To use SCPs as a whitelist, you must replace the AWS-managed `FullAWSAccess` SCP with an SCP that explicitly permits only those services and actions that you want to allow. By removing the default `FullAWSAccess` SCP, all actions for all services are now implicitly denied. Your custom SCP then overrides the implicit `Deny` with an explicit `Allow` for only those actions that you want to permit. Note that for a permission to be enabled for a specified account, every SCP from the root through each OU in the direct path to the account, and even attached to the account itself, must allow that permission.

Such a whitelist policy might look like the following example, which enables account users to perform operations for Amazon EC2 and Amazon CloudWatch, but no other service. All SCPs in parent OUs and the root also must explicitly allow these permissions:

```
1  {
2      "Version": "2012-10-17",
3      "Statement": [
4          {
5              "Effect": "Allow",
6              "Action": [
7                  "ec2:*",
8                  "cloudwatch:*"
9              ],
10             "Resource": "*"
11         }
12     ]
13 }
```

Example Service Control Policies

Important

The example service control policies (SCPs) displayed in this topic are for information purposes only. Before you attempt to use them in your organization, carefully review and customize them for your unique requirements. Remember that an SCP affects every user and role and even the root user in every account it's attached to. Test your policies before using them in a production capacity. Each of the following policies is an example of a blacklist policy strategy. Blacklist policies must be attached along with other policies that allow the approved actions in the affected accounts. For example, the default `FullAWSAccess` policy permits the use of all services in an account. This policy is attached by default to the root, all organizational units (OUs), and all accounts. It doesn't actually grant the permissions; no SCP does. Instead, it enables administrators in that account to delegate access to those actions by attaching standard IAM permission policies to users, roles, or groups in the account. Each of these blacklist policies then overrides any policy by blocking access to the specified services or actions.

Example 1: Prevent Users from Disabling AWS CloudTrail

This SCP prevents users or roles in any affected account from disabling a CloudTrail log, either directly as a command or through the console.

```
1  {
2    "Version": "2012-10-17",
3    "Statement": [
4      {
5        "Effect": "Deny",
6        "Action": "cloudtrail:StopLogging",
7        "Resource": "*"
8      }
9    ]
10 }
```

Example 2: Prevent Users from Disabling Amazon CloudWatch or Altering Its Configuration

A lower-level CloudWatch operator needs to monitor dashboards and alarms, but must not be able to delete or change any dashboard or alarm that senior people might put into place. This SCP prevents users or roles in any affected account from running any of the CloudWatch commands that could delete or change your dashboards or alarms.

```
1  {
2    "Version": "2012-10-17",
3    "Statement": [
4      {
5        "Effect": "Deny",
6        "Action": [
7          "cloudwatch:DeleteAlarms",
8          "cloudwatch:DeleteDashboards",
9          "cloudwatch:DisableAlarmActions",
10         "cloudwatch:PutDashboard",
11         "cloudwatch:PutMetricAlarm",
12         "cloudwatch:SetAlarmState"
13       ],
14       "Resource": "*"
```

```
15      }
16    ]
17 }
```

Example 3: Prevent Users from Deleting Amazon VPC Flow Logs

This SCP prevents users or roles in any affected account from deleting Amazon EC2 flow logs or CloudWatch log groups or log streams.

```
1  {
2    "Version": "2012-10-17",
3    "Statement": [
4      {
5        "Effect": "Deny",
6        "Action": [
7          "ec2:DeleteFlowLogs",
8          "logs:DeleteLogGroup",
9          "logs:DeleteLogStream"
10        ],
11        "Resource": "*"
12      }
13    ]
14  }
```

Example 4: Prevent Users from Disabling AWS Config or Changing Its Rules

This SCP prevents users or roles in any affected account from running AWS Config operations that could disable AWS Config or alter its rules or triggers.

```
1  {
2    "Version": "2012-10-17",
3    "Statement": [
4      {
5        "Effect": "Deny",
6        "Action": [
7          "config:DeleteConfigRule",
8          "config:DeleteConfigurationRecorder",
9          "config:DeleteDeliveryChannel",
10          "config:StopConfigurationRecorder"
11        ],
12        "Resource": "*"
13      }
14    ]
15  }
```

Example 5: Prevent Any VPC That Doesn't Already Have Internet Access from Getting It

This SCP prevents users or roles in any affected account from changing the configuration of your Amazon EC2 virtual private clouds (VPCs) to grant them direct access to the internet. It doesn't block existing direct access or any access that routes through your on-premises network environment.

```
 1  {
 2    "Version": "2012-10-17",
 3    "Statement": [
 4      {
 5        "Effect": "Deny",
 6        "Action": [
 7          "ec2:AttachInternetGateway",
 8          "ec2:CreateInternetGateway",
 9          "ec2:AttachEgressOnlyInternetGateway",
10          "ec2:CreateVpcPeeringConnection",
11          "ec2:AcceptVpcPeeringConnection"
12        ],
13        "Resource": "*"
14      }
15    ]
16  }
```

Enabling Trusted Access with Other AWS Services

You can use *trusted access* to enable an AWS service that you specify, called the *trusted service*, to perform tasks in your organization and its accounts on your behalf. This involves granting permissions to the trusted service but does *not* otherwise affect the permissions for IAM users or roles. When you enable access, the trusted service can create an IAM role called a *service-linked role* in every account in your organization. That role has a permissions policy that allows the trusted service to do the tasks that are described in that service's documentation. This enables you to specify settings and configuration details that you would like the trusted service to maintain in your organization's accounts on your behalf. The trusted service creates the roles asynchronously as needed, and not necessarily in all accounts of the organization.

Important
We recommend that you enable trusted access by using the trusted service's console, the AWS CLI, or the API operations in one of the AWS SDKs . This enables the trusted service to perform any required initialization or create any required resources. To learn what configuration the trusted service performs, see the documentation for that service.

Permissions Required to Enable Trusted Access

Trusted access requires permissions for two services: AWS Organizations and the trusted service. To enable trusted access, choose one of the following scenarios:

- If you have credentials that have permissions in both AWS Organizations and the trusted service, enable access by using the tools (console or AWS CLI) that are available in the trusted service. This allows the trusted service to enable trusted access in AWS Organizations on your behalf and to create any resources required for the service to operate in your organization.

  The minimum permissions for these credentials are the following:

  - `organizations:EnableAWSServiceAccess`. You can also use the `organizations:ServicePrincipal` condition key with this operation to limit requests that those operations make to a list of approved service principal names. For more information, see Condition Keys.
  - `organizations:ListAWSServiceAccessForOrganization` – Required if you use the AWS Organizations console.
  - The minimum permissions that are required by the trusted service depend on the service. For more information, see the trusted service's documentation.

- If one person has credentials with permissions in AWS Organizations but someone else has credentials with permissions in the trusted service, perform these steps in the following order:

  1. The person who has credentials with permissions in AWS Organizations should use the AWS Organizations console, the AWS CLI, or an AWS SDK to enable trusted access for the trusted service. This grants permission to the other service to perform its required configuration in the organization when the following step (step 2) is performed.

     The minimum AWS Organizations permissions are the following:

     - `organizations:EnableAWSServiceAccess`.
     - `organizations:ListAWSServiceAccessForOrganization` – Required only if you use the AWS Organizations console

     For the steps to enable trusted access in AWS Organizations, see How to Enable or Disable Trusted Access.

  2. The person who has credentials with permissions in the trusted service enables that service to work with AWS Organizations. This instructs the service to perform any required initialization, such as creating any resources that are required for the trusted service to operate in the organization. For

75

more information, see the service-specific instructions at Services That Support Trusted Access with Your Organization.

Permissions Required to Disable Trusted Access

When you no longer want to allow the trusted service to operate on your organization or its accounts, choose one of the following scenarios.

Important
Disabling trusted service access does ***not*** prevent users and roles with appropriate permissions from using that service. To completely block users and roles from accessing an AWS service, you can remove the IAM permissions that grant that access, or you can use service control policies (SCPs) in AWS Organizations.

- If you have credentials that have permissions in both AWS Organizations and the trusted service, disable access by using the tools (console or AWS CLI) that are available for the trusted service. The service then cleans up by removing resources that are no longer required and by disabling trusted access for the service in AWS Organizations on your behalf.

  The minimum permissions for these credentials are the following:

  - `organizations:DisableAWSServiceAccess`. You can also use the `organizations:ServicePrincipal` condition key with this operation to limit requests that those operations make to a list of approved service principal names. For more information, see Condition Keys.
  - `organizations:ListAWSServiceAccessForOrganization` – Required if you use the AWS Organizations console.
  - The minimum permissions required by the trusted service depend on the service. For more information, see the trusted service's documentation.

- If the credentials with permissions in AWS Organizations aren't the credentials with permissions in the trusted service, perform these steps in the following order:

  1. The person with permissions in the trusted service first disables access using that service. This instructs the trusted service to clean up by removing the resources required for trusted access. For more information, see the service-specific instructions at Services That Support Trusted Access with Your Organization.

  2. The person with permissions in AWS Organizations can then use the AWS Organizations console, AWS CLI, or an AWS SDK to disable access for the trusted service. This removes the permissions for the trusted service from the organization and its accounts.

     The minimum AWS Organizations permissions are the following:

     - `organizations:DisableAWSServiceAccess`.
     - `organizations:ListAWSServiceAccessForOrganization` – Required only if you use the AWS Organizations console

     For the steps to disable trusted access in AWS Organizations, see How to Enable or Disable Trusted Access.

How to Enable or Disable Trusted Access

If you have permissions only for AWS Organizations and you want to enable or disable trusted access to your organization on behalf of the administrator of the other AWS service, use the following procedure.

To enable or disable trusted service access (console)

1. Sign in to the Organizations console at https://console.aws.amazon.com/organizations/.

2. In the upper-right corner, choose **Settings**.

3. If you are *enabling* access, proceed to the next step. If you are *disabling* access, wait until the administrator tells you that the service is disabled and the resources have been cleaned up.

4. In the **Trusted access for AWS services** section, find the service that you want and then choose either **Enable access** or **Disable access** as appropriate.

5. If you are *enabling* access, tell the administrator of the other AWS service that they can now enable the other service to work with AWS Organizations.

To enable or disable trusted service access (AWS CLI, AWS API)

You can use the following AWS CLI commands or API operations to enable or disable trusted service access:

- AWS CLI: aws organizations enable-aws-service-access
- AWS CLI: aws organizations disable-aws-service-access
- AWS API: EnableAWSServiceAccess
- AWS API: DisableAWSServiceAccess

AWS Organizations and Service-Linked Roles

AWS Organizations uses IAM service-linked roles to enable trusted services to perform tasks on your behalf in your organization's member accounts. When you configure a trusted service and authorize it to integrate with your organization, that service can request that AWS Organizations create a service-linked role in its member account. The trusted service does this asynchronously as needed and not necessarily in all accounts in the organization at the same time. The service-linked role has predefined IAM permissions that allow the trusted service to perform specific tasks within that account. In general, AWS manages all service-linked roles, which means that you typically can't alter the roles or the attached policies.

To make all of this possible, when you create an account in an organization or you accept an invitation to join your existing account to an organization, AWS Organizations provisions the account with a service-linked role named AWSServiceRoleForOrganizations. Only the AWS Organizations service itself can assume this role. The role has permissions that allow only AWS Organizations to create service-linked roles for other AWS services. This service-linked role is present in all organizations.

Although we don't recommend it, if your organization has only consolidated billing features enabled, the service-linked role named AWSServiceRoleForOrganizations is never used, and you can delete it. If you later want to enable all features in your organization, the role is required, and you must restore it. The following checks occur when you begin the process to enable all features:

- **For each member account that was *invited to join* the organization** – The account administrator receives a request to agree to enable all features. To successfully agree to the request, the administrator must have both organizations:AcceptHandshake and iam:CreateServiceLinkedRole permissions if the service-linked role (AWSServiceRoleForOrganizations) doesn't already exist. If the AWSServiceRoleForOrganizations role already exists, the administrator needs only the organizations: AcceptHandshake permission to agree to the request. When the administrator agrees to the request, AWS Organizations creates the service-linked role if it doesn't already exist.
- **For each member account that was *created* in the organization** – The account administrator receives a request to recreate the service-linked role. (The administrator of the member account doesn't receive a request to enable all features because the administrator of the master account is considered the owner of the created member accounts.) AWS Organizations creates the service-linked role when the member account administrator agrees to the request. The administrator must have both organizations: AcceptHandshake and iam:CreateServiceLinkedRole permissions to successfully accept the handshake.

After you enable all features in your organization, you no longer can delete the AWSServiceRoleForOrganizations service-linked role from any account.

Important
AWS Organizations SCPs never affect service-linked roles. These roles are exempt from any SCP restrictions.

Services That Support Trusted Access with Your Organization

The following sections describe the AWS services for which you can enable trusted access with your organization. Each section includes the following:

- A summary of the trusted service and how it works when you enable trusted access
- Links to instructions for enabling and disabling trusted access with your organization
- The principal name of the trusted service that you can specify in policies to grant the trusted access to the accounts in your organization
- If applicable, the name of the IAM service-linked role created in all accounts when you enable trusted access

AWS Artifact

AWS Artifact is a service that allows you to download AWS security compliance reports such as ISO and PCI reports. Using AWS Artifact, a user in a master account can automatically accept agreements on behalf of all member accounts in an organization, even as new reports and accounts are added. Member account users can view and download agreements. For more information about AWS Artifact, see the AWS Artifact User Guide.

The following list provides information that is useful to know when you want to integrate AWS Artifact and Organizations:

- **To enable trusted access with Organizations:** You must sign in with your AWS Organizations master account to configure an account within the organization as the AWS Artifact administrator account. For information, see Step 1: Create an Admin Group and Add an IAM User in the *AWS Artifact User Guide*.

- **To disable trusted access with Organizations:** AWS Artifact requires trusted access with AWS Organizations to work with organization agreements. If you disable trusted access using Organizations while you are using AWS Artifact for organization agreements, it stops functioning because it cannot access the organization. Any organization agreements that you accept in AWS Artifact remain, but can't be accessed by AWS Artifact. The AWS Artifact role that AWS Artifact creates remains. If you then re-enable trusted access, AWS Artifact continues to operate as before, without the need for you to reconfigure the service.

  A standalone account that is removed from an organization no longer has access to any organization agreements.

- **Service principal name for AWS Artifact:** aws-artifact-account-sync.amazonaws.com

- **Role name created to synchronize with AWS Artifact:** AWSArtifactAccountSync

AWS Config

Multi-account, multi-region data aggregation in AWS Config allows you to aggregate AWS Config data from multiple accounts and regions into a single account. Multi-account, multi-region data aggregation is useful for central IT administrators to monitor compliance for multiple AWS accounts in the enterprise. An aggregator is a new resource type in AWS Config that collects AWS Config data from multiple source accounts and regions. Create an aggregator in the region where you want to see the aggregated AWS Config data. While creating an aggregator, you can choose to add either individual account IDs or your organization. For more information about AWS Config, see the AWS Config Developer Guide.

The following list provides information that is useful to know when you want to integrate AWS Config and AWS Organizations:

- **To enable trusted access with AWS Organizations:** To enable trusted access to AWS Organizations from AWS Config, you create a multi-account aggregator and add the organization. For information on how to configure a multi-account aggregator, see Setting Up an Aggregator Using the Console in the *AWS Config Developer Guide*.

- **Service principal name for AWS Config**: `config.amazonaws.com`.
- **Name of the IAM service-linked role that can be created in accounts** when trusted access is enabled: `AWSConfigRoleForOrganizations`.

AWS Firewall Manager

AWS Firewall Manager is a security management service that centrally configures and manages firewall rules for web applications across your accounts and applications. Using AWS Firewall Manager, you can roll out AWS WAF rules all at once for your Application Load Balancers and Amazon CloudFront distributions across all of the accounts in your AWS organization. Use AWS Firewall Manager to set up your firewall rules just once and have them automatically applied across all accounts and resources within your organization, even as new resources and accounts are added. For more information about AWS Firewall Manager, see the AWS Firewall Developer Guide.

The following list provides information that is useful to know when you want to integrate AWS Firewall Manager and AWS Organizations:

- **To enable trusted access with AWS Organizations:** You must sign in with your AWS Organizations master account to configure an account within the organization as the AWS Firewall Manager administrator account. For information, see Step 2: Set the AWS Firewall Manager Administrator Account in the *AWS Firewall Manager Developer Guide.*
- **To disable trusted access with AWS Organizations:** You can change or revoke the AWS Firewall Manager administrator account by following the instructions in Designating a Different Account as the AWS Firewall Manager Administrator Account in the *AWS Firewall Manager Developer Guide.* If you revoke the administrator account, you must sign in to the AWS Organizations master account and set a new administrator account for AWS Firewall Manager.
- **Service principal name for AWS Firewall Manager:** `fms.amazonaws.com`
- **Name of the IAM service-linked role that can be created in accounts** when trusted access is enabled: `AWSServiceRoleForFMS`

AWS Single Sign-On

AWS Single Sign-On (AWS SSO) provides single sign-on services for all of your AWS accounts and cloud applications. It connects with Microsoft Active Directory through AWS Directory Service to allow users in that directory to sign in to a personalized user portal using their existing Active Directory user names and passwords. From the portal, users have access to all the AWS accounts and cloud applications that you provide in the portal. For more information about AWS SSO, see the AWS Single Sign-On User Guide.

The following list provides information that is useful to know when you want to integrate AWS SSO and AWS Organizations:

- **To enable trusted access with AWS Organizations:** AWS SSO requires trusted access with AWS Organizations to function. Trusted access is enabled when you set up AWS SSO. For more information, see Getting Started - Step 1: Enable AWS Single Sign-On in the *AWS Single Sign-On User Guide.*

- **To disable trusted access with AWS Organizations:** AWS SSO requires trusted access with AWS Organizations to operate. If you disable trusted access using AWS Organizations while you are using AWS SSO, it stops functioning because it can't access the organization. Users can't use AWS SSO to access accounts. Any roles that AWS SSO creates remain, but the AWS SSO service can't access them. The AWS SSO service-linked roles remain. If you reenable trusted access, AWS SSO continues to operate as before, without the need for you to reconfigure the service.

  If you remove an account from your organization, AWS SSO automatically cleans up any metadata and resources, such as its service-linked role. A standalone account that is removed from an organization no longer works with AWS SSO.

- **Service principal name for AWS SSO:** `sso.amazonaws.com`

- **Name of the IAM service-linked role that can be created in accounts** when trusted access is enabled: `AWSServiceRoleForSSO`

  For more information, see Using Service-Linked Roles for AWS SSO in the *AWS Single Sign-On User Guide.*

Authentication and Access Control for AWS Organizations

Access to AWS Organizations requires credentials. Those credentials must have permissions to access AWS resources, such as an Amazon Simple Storage Service (Amazon S3) bucket, an Amazon Elastic Compute Cloud (Amazon EC2) instance, or an AWS Organizations organizational unit (OU). The following sections provide details on how you can use AWS Identity and Access Management (IAM) to help secure access to your organization and control who can administer it.

To determine who can administer which parts of your organization, AWS Organizations uses the same IAM-based permissions model as other AWS services. As an administrator in the master account of an organization, you can grant IAM-based permissions to perform AWS Organizations tasks by attaching policies to users, groups, and roles in the master account. Those policies specify the actions that those principals can perform. You attach an IAM permissions policy to a group that the user is a member of or directly to a user or role. As a best practice, we recommend that you attach policies to groups instead of users. You also have the option to grant full administrator permissions to others.

For most administrator operations for AWS Organizations, you need to attach permissions to users or groups in the master account. If a user in a member account needs to perform administrator operations for your organization, you need to grant the AWS Organizations permissions to an *IAM role* in the master account and enable the user in the member account to assume the role. For general information about IAM permissions policies, see Overview of IAM Policies in the *IAM User Guide*.

Topics

- Authentication
- Access Control
- Managing Access Permissions for Your AWS Organization
- Using Identity-Based Policies (IAM Policies) for AWS Organizations

Authentication

You can access AWS as any of the following types of identities:

- **AWS account root user** – When you sign up for AWS, you provide an email address and password that is associated with your AWS account. These are your *root credentials*, and they provide complete access to all of your AWS resources. **Important**
  For security reasons, we recommend that you use the root credentials only to create an *administrator user*, which is an *IAM user* with full permissions to your AWS account. Then you can use this administrator user to create other IAM users and roles with limited permissions. For more information, see IAM Best Practices and Creating Your First IAM Admin User and Group in the *IAM User Guide*.

- **IAM user** – An IAM user is simply an identity within your AWS account that has specific custom permissions (for example, permissions to create a file system in Amazon Elastic File System). You can use an IAM user name and password to sign in to secure AWS webpages like the AWS Management Console, AWS Discussion Forums, or the AWS Support Center.

  In addition to a user name and password, you can generate access keys for each user. You can use these keys when you access AWS services programmatically, either through one of the several SDKs or by using the AWS Command Line Interface (AWS CLI). The SDK and AWS CLI tools use the access keys to cryptographically sign your request. If you don't use the AWS tools, you must sign the request yourself. AWS Organizations supports *Signature Version 4*, a protocol for authenticating inbound API requests. For more information about authenticating requests, see Signature Version 4 Signing Process in the *AWS General Reference*.

- **IAM role** – An IAM role is another IAM identity you can create in your account that has specific permissions. It is similar to an IAM user, but it isn't associated with a specific person. An IAM role allows you to obtain temporary access keys that can access AWS services and resources. IAM roles with temporary credentials are useful in the following situations:

- **Federated user access** – Instead of creating an IAM user, you can use preexisting user identities from AWS Directory Service, your enterprise user directory, or a web identity provider. These are known as *federated users*. AWS assigns a role to a federated user when access is requested through an identity provider. For more information about federated users, see Federated Users and Roles in the *IAM User Guide*.
- **Cross-account access** – You can use an IAM role in your account to grant another AWS account permissions to access your account's resources. For an example, see Tutorial: Delegate Access Across AWS Accounts Using IAM Roles in the *IAM User Guide*.
- **AWS service access** – You can use an IAM role in your account to grant an AWS service permissions to access your account's resources. For example, you can create a role that allows Amazon Redshift to access an Amazon S3 bucket on your behalf and then load data stored in the bucket into an Amazon Redshift cluster. For more information, see Creating a Role to Delegate Permissions to an AWS Service in the *IAM User Guide*.
- **Applications running on Amazon EC2** – Instead of storing access keys in the EC2 instance for use by applications running on the instance and making AWS API requests, you can use an IAM role to manage temporary credentials for these applications. To assign an AWS role to an EC2 instance and make it available to all of its applications, you can create an instance profile that is attached to the instance. An instance profile contains the role and enables programs running on the EC2 instance to get temporary credentials. For more information, see Using Roles for Applications on Amazon EC2 in the *IAM User Guide*.

Access Control

You can have valid credentials to authenticate your requests, but unless you have permissions, you can't administer or access AWS Organizations resources. For example, you must have permissions to create an OU or to attach a service control policy (SCP) to an account.

The following sections describe how to manage permissions for AWS Organizations. We recommend that you read the overview first.

- Managing Access Permissions for Your AWS Organization
- Using Identity-Based Policies (IAM Policies) for AWS Organizations

Managing Access Permissions for Your AWS Organization

All AWS resources, including the roots, OUs, accounts, and policies in an organization, are owned by an AWS account, and permissions to create or access a resource are governed by permissions policies. In the case of an organization, its master account owns all resources. An account administrator can control access to AWS resources by attaching permissions policies to IAM identities (users, groups, and roles).

Note
An *account administrator* (or administrator user) is a user with administrator permissions. For more information, see IAM Best Practices in the *IAM User Guide*.

When granting permissions, you decide who is getting the permissions, the resources that they get permissions for, and the specific actions that you want to allow on those resources.

By default, IAM users, groups, and roles have no permissions. As an administrator in the master account of an organization, you can perform administrative tasks or delegate administrator permissions to other IAM users or roles in the master account. To do this, you attach an IAM permissions policy to an IAM user, group, or role. By default, a user has no permissions at all; this is sometimes called an *implicit deny*. The policy overrides the implicit deny with an *explicit allow* that specifies which actions the user can perform, and which resources they can perform the actions on. If the permissions are granted to a role, users in other accounts in the organization can assume that role.

AWS Organizations Resources and Operations

This section discusses how AWS Organizations concepts map to their IAM-equivalent concepts.

Resources

In AWS Organizations, you can control access to the following resources:

- The root and the OUs that make up the hierarchical structure of an organization
- The accounts that are members of the organization
- The policies that you attach to the entities in the organization
- The handshakes that you use to change the state of the organization

Each of these resources has a unique Amazon Resource Name (ARN) associated with it. You control access to a resource by specifying its ARN in the `Resource` element of an IAM permission policy. For a complete list of the ARN formats for resources that are used in AWS Organizations, see Resources Defined by AWS Organizations in the *IAM User Guide*.

Operations

AWS provides a set of operations to work with the resources in an organization. They enable you to do things like create, list, modify, access the contents of, and delete resources. Most operations can be referenced in the `Action` element of an IAM policy to control who can use that operation. For a list of AWS Organizations operations that can be used as permissions in an IAM policy, see API Action Permissions Defined by AWS Organizations in the *IAM User Guide*.

When you combine an `Action` and a `Resource` in a single permission policy `Statement`, you control exactly which resources that particular set of actions can be used on.

Condition Keys

AWS provides condition keys that you can query to provide more granular control over certain actions. You can reference these condition keys in the `Condition` element of an IAM policy to specify the additional circumstances that must be met for the statement to be considered a match.

The following condition keys are especially useful with AWS Organizations:

- `organizations:ServicePrincipal` – Available as a condition if you use the EnableAWSServiceAccess or DisableAWSServiceAccess operations to enable or disable trusted access with other AWS services. You can use `organizations:ServicePrincipal` to limit requests that those operations make to a list of approved service principal names.

  For example, the following policy allows the user to specify only AWS Firewall Manager when enabling and disabling trusted access with AWS Organizations:

```
1  {
2      "Version": "2012-10-17",
3      "Statement": [
4          {
5              "Sid": "AllowOnlyAWSFirewallIntegration",
6              "Effect": "Allow",
7              "Action": [
8                  "organizations:EnableAWSServiceAccess",
9                  "organizations:DisableAWSServiceAccess"
10             ],
11             "Resource": "*",
12             "Condition": {
13                 "ForAllValues:StringLike": {
14                     "organizations:ServicePrincipal": [ "fms.amazonaws.com" ]
15                 }
16             }
17         }
18     ]
19 }
```

- `aws:PrincipalOrgID` – Simplifies specifying the `Principal` element in a resource-based policy. This global key provides an alternative to listing all the account IDs for all AWS accounts in an organization. Instead of listing all of the accounts that are members of an organization, you can specify the organization ID in the `Condition` element. **Note**
  This global condition also applies to the master account of an AWS organization.

  For more information, see the description of `PrincipalOrgID` in AWS Global Condition Context Keys in the *IAM User Guide*.

For a list of all of the AWS Organizations–specific condition keys that can be used as permissions in an IAM policy, see Condition Context Keys for AWS Organizations in the *IAM User Guide*.

Understanding Resource Ownership

The AWS account owns the resources that are created in the account, regardless of who created the resources. Specifically, the resource owner is the AWS account of the principal entity (that is, the root account, an IAM user, or an IAM role) that authenticates the resource creation request. For an AWS organization, that is ***always*** the master account. You can't call most operations that create or access organization resources from the member accounts. The following examples illustrate how this works:

- If you use the root account credentials of your master account to create an OU, your master account is the owner of the resource. (In AWS Organizations, the resource is the OU.)
- If you create an IAM user in your master account and grant permissions to create an OU to that user, the user can create an OU. However, the master account, to which the user belongs, owns the OU resource.
- If you create an IAM role in your master account with permissions to create an OU, anyone who can assume the role can create an OU. The master account, to which the role (not the assuming user) belongs, owns the OU resource.

Managing Access to Resources

A *permissions policy* describes who has access to what. The following section explains the available options for creating permissions policies.

Note

This section discusses using IAM in the context of AWS Organizations. It doesn't provide detailed information about the IAM service. For complete IAM documentation, see the IAM User Guide. For information about IAM policy syntax and descriptions, see the AWS IAM Policy Reference in the *IAM User Guide.*

Policies that are attached to an IAM identity are referred to as *identity-based* policies (IAM policies). Policies that are attached to a resource are referred to as *resource-based* policies. AWS Organizations supports only identity-based policies (IAM policies).

Topics

- Identity-based Policies (IAM Policies)
- Resource-based Policies

Identity-based Policies (IAM Policies)

You can attach policies to IAM identities. For example, you can do the following:

- **Attach a permissions policy to a user or a group in your account** – To grant a user permissions to create an AWS Organizations resource, such as a service control policy (SCP) or an OU, you can attach a permissions policy to a user or a group that the user belongs to. The user or group must be in the organization's master account.

- **Attach a permissions policy to a role (grant cross-account permissions)** – You can attach an identity-based permissions policy to an IAM role to grant cross-account access to an organization. For example, the administrator in the master account can create a role to grant cross-account permissions to a user in a member account as follows:

  1. The master account administrator creates an IAM role and attaches a permissions policy to the role that grants permissions to the organization's resources.

  2. The master account administrator attaches a trust policy to the role that identifies the member account ID as the `Principal` who can assume the role.

  3. The member account administrator can then delegate permissions to assume the role to any users in the member account. Doing this allows users in the member account to create or access resources in the master account and the organization. The principal in the trust policy can also be an AWS service principal if you want to grant permissions to an AWS service to assume the role.

  For more information about using IAM to delegate permissions, see Access Management in the *IAM User Guide.*

The following is an example policy that allows a user to perform the `CreateAccount` action in your organization:

```
1 {
2   "Version": "2012-10-17",
```

```
3    "Statement": [
4      {
5        "Sid" : "Stmt1OrgPermissions",
6        "Effect": "Allow",
7        "Action": [
8          "organizations:CreateAccount"
9        ],
10       "Resource": "*"
11     }
12   ]
```

For more information about using identity-based policies, see Using Identity-Based Policies (IAM Policies) for AWS Organizations. For more information about users, groups, roles, and permissions, see Identities (Users, Groups, and Roles) in the *IAM User Guide*.

Resource-based Policies

Some services, such as Amazon S3, support resource-based permissions policies. For example, you can attach a policy to an Amazon S3 bucket to manage access permissions to that bucket. AWS Organizations currently doesn't support resource-based policies.

Specifying Policy Elements: Actions, Conditions, Effects, and Resources

For each AWS Organizations resource, the service defines a set of API operations, or actions, that can interact with or manipulate that resource in some way. To grant permissions for these operations, AWS Organizations defines a set of actions that you can specify in a policy. For example, for the OU resource, AWS Organizations defines actions like the following:

- AttachPolicy and DetachPolicy
- CreateOrganizationalUnit and DeleteOrganizationalUnit
- ListOrganizationalUnits and DescribeOrganizationalUnit

In some cases, performing an API operation might require permissions to more than one action and might require permissions to more than one resource.

The following are the most basic elements that you can use in an IAM permission policy:

- **Action** – Use this keyword to identify the operations (actions) that you want to allow or deny. For example, depending on the specified Effect, organizations:CreateAccount allows or denies the user permissions to perform the AWS Organizations CreateAccount operation. For more information, see IAM JSON Policy Elements: Action in the *IAM User Guide*.
- **Resource** – Use this keyword to specify the ARN of the resource to which the policy statement applies. For more information, see IAM JSON Policy Elements: Resource in the *IAM User Guide*.
- **Condition** – Use this keyword to specify a condition that must be met for the policy statement to apply. Condition usually specifies additional circumstances that must be true for the policy to match. For more information, see IAM JSON Policy Elements: Condition in the *IAM User Guide*.
- **Effect** – Use this keyword to specify whether the policy statement allows or denies the action on the resource. If you don't explicitly grant access to (or allow) a resource, access is implicitly denied. You also can explicitly deny access to a resource, which you might do to ensure that a user can't perform the specified action on the specified resource, even if a different policy grants access. For more information, see IAM JSON Policy Elements: Effect in the *IAM User Guide*.
- **Principal** – In identity-based policies (IAM policies), the user that the policy is attached to is automatically and implicitly the principal. For resource-based policies, you specify the user, account, service, or other entity that you want to receive permissions (applies to resource-based policies only). AWS Organizations currently supports only identity-based policies, not resource-based policies.

To learn more about IAM policy syntax and descriptions, see the AWS IAM Policy Reference in the *IAM User Guide*.

For a table that show all of the AWS Organizations API actions that can be used in IAM policies, see Using Identity-Based Policies (IAM Policies) for AWS Organizations.

Using Identity-Based Policies (IAM Policies) for AWS Organizations

As an administrator of the master account of an organization, you can control access to AWS resources by attaching permissions policies to AWS Identity and Access Management (IAM) identities (users, groups, and roles) within the organization. When granting permissions, you decide who is getting the permissions, the resources they get permissions for, and the specific actions that you want to allow on those resources. If the permissions are granted to a role, that role can be assumed by users in other accounts in the organization.

By default, a user has no permissions of any kind. All permissions must be explicitly granted by a policy. If a permission isn't explicitly granted, it's implicitly denied. If a permission is explicitly denied, that overrules any other policy that might have allowed it. In other words, a user has only those permissions that are explicitly granted and that aren't explicitly denied.

Granting Full Admin Permissions to a User

You can create an IAM policy that grants full AWS Organizations administrator permissions to an IAM user in your organization. You can do this using the JSON policy editor in the IAM console.

To use the JSON policy editor to create a policy

1. Sign in to the AWS Management Console and open the IAM console at https://console.aws.amazon.com/iam/.

2. In the navigation column on the left, choose **Policies**.

   If this is your first time choosing **Policies**, the **Welcome to Managed Policies** page appears. Choose **Get Started**.

3. At the top of the page, choose **Create policy**.

4. Choose the **JSON** tab.

5. Type the following JSON policy document:

```
1 {
2   "Version": "2012-10-17",
3   "Statement": {
4     "Effect": "Allow",
5     "Action": "organizations:*",
6     "Resource": "*"
7   }
8 }
```

6. Choose **Review policy**. **Note**
   You can switch between the **Visual editor** and **JSON** tabs any time. However, if you make changes or choose **Review policy** in the **Visual editor** tab, IAM might restructure your policy to optimize it for the visual editor. For more information, see Policy Restructuring in the *IAM User Guide*.

7. On the **Review policy** page, type a **Name** and a **Description** (optional) for the policy that you are creating. Review the policy **Summary** to see the permissions that are granted by your policy. Then choose **Create policy** to save your work.

To learn more about creating an IAM policy, see Creating IAM Policies in the *IAM User Guide*.

Granting Limited Access by Actions

If you want to grant limited permissions instead of full permissions, you can create a policy that lists individual permissions that you want to allow in the `Action` element of the IAM permissions policy. As shown in the following example, you can use wildcard (*) characters to grant only the `Describe*` and `List*` permissions, essentially providing read-only access to the organization.

Note
In a service control policy (SCP), the wildcard (*) character in an `Action` element can be used only by itself or at the end of the string. It can't appear at the beginning or middle of the string. Therefore, `"servicename:action*"` is valid, but `"servicename:*action"` and `"servicename:some*action"` are both invalid in SCPs.

```
1  {
2     "Version": "2012-10-17",
3     "Statement": {
4       "Effect": "Allow",
5       "Action": [
6         "organizations:Describe*",
7         "organizations:List*"
8       ],
9       "Resource": "*"
10    }
11 }
```

For a list of all the permissions that are available to assign in an IAM policy, see Actions Defined by AWS Organizations in the *IAM User Guide*.

Granting Access to Specific Resources

In addition to restricting access to specific actions, you can restrict access to specific entities in your organization. The `Resource` elements in the examples in the preceding sections both specify the wildcard character ("*"), which means "any resource that the action can access." Instead, you can replace the "*" with the Amazon Resource Name (ARN) of specific entities to which you want to allow access.

Example: Granting permissions to a single OU
The first statement of the following policy allows an IAM user read access to the entire organization, but the second statement allows the user to perform AWS Organizations administrative actions only within a single, specified organizational unit (OU). No billing access is granted. Note that this doesn't give you administrative access to the accounts in the OU. It grants only permissions to perform AWS Organizations operations on the accounts and child OUs within the specified OU:

```
1  {
2    "Version": "2012-10-17",
3    "Statement": [
4      {
5        "Effect": "Allow",
6        "Action": [
7          "organizations:Describe*",
8          "organizations:List*"
9        ],
10       "Resource": "*"
11     },
12     {
13       "Effect": "Allow",
14       "Action": "organizations:*",
15       "Resource": "arn:aws:organizations::<masterAccountId>:ou/o-<organizationId>/ou-<
              organizationalUnitId>"
16     }
17   ]
18 }
```

You get the IDs for the OU and the organization from the AWS Organizations console or by calling the `List*` APIs. The user or group that you apply this policy to can perform any action (`"organizations:*"`) on any entity that is contained by the OU. The OU is identified by the Amazon Resource Name (ARN).

For more information about the ARNs for various resources, see Resources Defined by AWS Organizations in the *IAM User Guide.*

Granting the Ability to Enable Trusted Access to Limited Service Principals

You can use the `Condition` element of a policy statement to further limit the circumstances where the policy statement matches.

Example: Granting permissions to enable trusted access to one specified service
The following statement shows how you can restrict the ability to enable trusted access to only those services that you specify. If the user tries to call the API with a different service principal than the one for AWS Single Sign-On, this policy doesn't match and the request is denied:

```
1  {
2      "Version": "2012-10-17",
3      "Statement": [
4        {
5          "Effect": "Allow",
6          "Action": "organizations:EnableAWSServiceAccess",
7          "Resource": "*",
8          "Condition": {
9            "StringEquals" : {
10              "organizations:ServicePrincipal" : "sso.amazonaws.com"
11           }
12         }
13       }
14     ]
15  }
```

For more information about the ARNs for various resources, see Resources Defined by AWS Organizations in the *IAM User Guide.*

Monitoring the Activity in Your Organization

As a best practice, you should monitor your organization to ensure that changes are logged. This helps you to ensure that any unexpected change can be investigated and unwanted changes can be rolled back. AWS Organizations currently supports two AWS services that enable you to monitor your organization and the activity that happens within it.

Topics

- AWS CloudTrail
- Amazon CloudWatch Events

AWS CloudTrail

AWS Organizations is integrated with AWS CloudTrail, a service that captures AWS Organizations API calls and delivers the log files to an Amazon Simple Storage Service (Amazon S3) bucket that you specify. CloudTrail captures API calls from the AWS Organizations console or from your code. Using the information collected by CloudTrail, you can determine the request that was made to AWS Organizations, the source IP address from which the request was made, who made the request, when it was made, and so on.

AWS Organizations is also integrated with the **Event history** feature in CloudTrail. If an API for AWS Organizations is supported in **Event history**, you can view the most recent 90 days of events in AWS Organizations in the CloudTrail console in **Event history** even if you have not configured any logs in CloudTrail.

Important
You can view all CloudTrail information for AWS Organizations only in the US East (N. Virginia) Region. If you don't see your AWS Organizations activity in the CloudTrail console, set your console to **US East (N. Virginia)** using the menu in the upper-right corner. If you query CloudTrail with the AWS CLI or SDK tools, direct your query to the US East (N. Virginia) endpoint.

To learn more about CloudTrail, including how to configure and enable it, see the AWS CloudTrail User Guide.

AWS Organizations Information in CloudTrail

CloudTrail is enabled on your AWS account when you create the account. When activity occurs in AWS Organizations, that activity is recorded in a CloudTrail event along with other AWS service events in **Event history**. You can view, search, and download the past 90 days of supported activity in your AWS account. For more information, see Viewing Events with CloudTrail Event History and Services Supported by CloudTrail Event History.

When CloudTrail logging is enabled in your AWS account, API calls made to AWS Organizations actions are tracked in CloudTrail log files, where they are written with other AWS service records. CloudTrail determines when to create and write to a new file based on a time period and file size.

All AWS Organizations actions are logged by CloudTrail and are documented in the AWS Organizations API Reference. For example, calls to the `ListHandshakesForAccount`, `CreatePolicy`, and `InviteAccountToOrganization` operations generate entries in the CloudTrail log files.

Every log entry contains information about who generated the request. The user identity information in the log entry helps you determine the following:

- Whether the request was made with root or IAM user credentials
- Whether the request was made with temporary security credentials for an IAM role or a federated user whose security credentials are validated by an external identity provider instead of directly by AWS
- Whether the request was made by another AWS service

For more information, see the CloudTrail userIdentity Element.

You can store your log files in your Amazon S3 bucket for as long as you want, but you can also define Amazon S3 lifecycle rules to archive or delete log files automatically. By default, your log files are encrypted with Amazon S3 server-side encryption (SSE).

If you want to be notified upon log file delivery, you can configure CloudTrail to publish Amazon Simple Notification Service (Amazon SNS) notifications when new log files are delivered. For more information, see Configuring Amazon SNS Notifications for CloudTrail.

Understanding AWS Organizations Log File Entries

CloudTrail log files can contain one or more log entries. Each entry lists multiple JSON-formatted events. A log entry represents a single request from any source and includes information about the requested action, the date and time of the action, request parameters, and so on. Log entries aren't an ordered stack trace of the public API calls, so they don't appear in any specific order.

The following example shows a CloudTrail log entry for a sample `CreateAccount` call:

```
{
    "eventVersion": "1.04",
    "userIdentity": {
        "type": "IAMUser",
        "principalId": "AIDAMVNPBQA3EXAMPLE",
        "arn": "arn:aws:iam::111122223333:user/bob",
        "accountId": "111122223333",
        "accessKeyId": "AKIAIOSFODNN7EXAMPLE",
        "userName": "bob"
    },
    "eventTime": "2017-01-18T21:39:20Z",
    "eventSource": "organizations.amazonaws.com",
    "eventName": "CreateAccount",
    "awsRegion": "us-east-1",
    "sourceIPAddress": "192.168.0.1",
    "userAgent": "Mozilla/5.0 (Macintosh; Intel Mac OS X 10_11_6) AppleWebKit/537.36 (KHTML,
        like Gecko) Chrome/55.0.2883.95 Safari/537.36",
    "requestParameters": {
        "email": "anika@amazon.com",
        "accountName": "ProductionAccount"
    },
    "responseElements": {
        "createAccountStatus": {
            "accountName": "ProductionAccount",
            "state": "IN_PROGRESS",
            "id": "car-examplecreateaccountrequestid111",
            "requestedTimestamp": "Jan 18, 2017 9:39:19 PM"
        }
    },
    "requestID": "EXAMPLE8-90ab-cdef-fedc-ba987EXAMPLE",
    "eventID": "EXAMPLE8-90ab-cdef-fedc-ba987EXAMPLE",
    "eventType": "AwsApiCall",
    "recipientAccountId": "111111111111"
}
```

The following example shows a CloudTrail log entry for a sample `CreateOrganizationalUnit` call:

```json
{
    "eventVersion": "1.04",
    "userIdentity": {
        "type": "IAMUser",
        "principalId": "AIDAMVNPBQA3EXAMPLE",
        "arn": "arn:aws:iam::111111111111:user/bob",
        "accountId": "111111111111",
        "accessKeyId": "AKIAIOSFODNN7EXAMPLE",
        "userName": "bob"
    },
    "eventTime": "2017-01-18T21:40:11Z",
    "eventSource": "organizations.amazonaws.com",
    "eventName": "CreateOrganizationalUnit",
    "awsRegion": "us-east-1",
    "sourceIPAddress": "192.168.0.1",
    "userAgent": "Mozilla/5.0 (Macintosh; Intel Mac OS X 10_11_6) AppleWebKit/537.36 (KHTML,
        like Gecko) Chrome/55.0.2883.95 Safari/537.36",
    "requestParameters": {
        "name": "OU-Developers-1",
        "parentId": "r-examplerootid111"
    },
    "responseElements": {
        "organizationalUnit": {
            "arn": "arn:aws:organizations::111111111111:ou/o-exampleorgid/ou-examplerootid111-
                exampleouid111",
            "id": "ou-examplerootid111-exampleouid111",
            "name": "test-cloud-trail"
        }
    },
    "requestID": "EXAMPLE8-90ab-cdef-fedc-ba987EXAMPLE",
    "eventID": "EXAMPLE8-90ab-cdef-fedc-ba987EXAMPLE",
    "eventType": "AwsApiCall",
    "recipientAccountId": "111111111111"
}
```

The following example shows a CloudTrail log entry for a sample InviteAccountToOrganization call:

```json
{
    "eventVersion": "1.04",
    "userIdentity": {
        "type": "IAMUser",
        "principalId": "AIDAMVNPBQA3EXAMPLE",
        "arn": "arn:aws:iam::111111111111:user/bob",
        "accountId": "111111111111",
        "accessKeyId": "AKIAIOSFODNN7EXAMPLE",
        "userName": "bob"
    },
    "eventTime": "2017-01-18T21:41:17Z",
    "eventSource": "organizations.amazonaws.com",
    "eventName": "InviteAccountToOrganization",
    "awsRegion": "us-east-1",
    "sourceIPAddress": "192.168.0.1",
    "userAgent": "Mozilla/5.0 (Macintosh; Intel Mac OS X 10_11_6) AppleWebKit/537.36 (KHTML,
        like Gecko) Chrome/55.0.2883.95 Safari/537.36",
    "requestParameters": {
```

```
18      "notes": "This is a request for Alice's account to join Bob's organization.",
19      "target": {
20          "type": "ACCOUNT",
21          "id": "222222222222"
22      }
23  },
24  "responseElements": {
25      "handshake": {
26          "requestedTimestamp": "Jan 18, 2017 9:41:16 PM",
27          "state": "OPEN",
28          "arn": "arn:aws:organizations::111111111111:handshake/o-exampleorgid/invite/h-
                examplehandshakeid111",
29          "id": "h-examplehandshakeid111",
30          "parties": [
31              {
32                  "type": "ORGANIZATION",
33                  "id": "o-exampleorgid"
34              },
35              {
36                  "type": "ACCOUNT",
37                  "id": "222222222222"
38              }
39          ],
40          "action": "invite",
41          "expirationTimestamp": "Feb 2, 2017 9:41:16 PM",
42          "resources": [
43              {
44                  "resources": [
45                      {
46                          "type": "MASTER_EMAIL",
47                          "value": "bob@example.com"
48                      },
49                      {
50                          "type": "MASTER_NAME",
51                          "value": "Master account for organization"
52                      },
53                      {
54                          "type": "ORGANIZATION_FEATURE_SET",
55                          "value": "ALL"
56                      }
57                  ],
58                  "type": "ORGANIZATION",
59                  "value": "o-exampleorgid"
60              },
61              {
62                  "type": "ACCOUNT",
63                  "value": "222222222222"
64              },
65              {
66                  "type": "NOTES",
67                  "value": "This is a request for Alice's account to join Bob's organization."
68              }
69          ]
70      }
```

94

```
71        },
72        "requestID": "EXAMPLE8-90ab-cdef-fedc-ba987EXAMPLE",
73        "eventID": "EXAMPLE8-90ab-cdef-fedc-ba987EXAMPLE",
74        "eventType": "AwsApiCall",
75        "recipientAccountId": "111111111111"
76 }
```

The following example shows a CloudTrail log entry for a sample `AttachPolicy` call. The response indicates that the call failed because the requested policy type isn't enabled in the root where the request to attach was attempted:

```
1  {
2        "eventVersion": "1.04",
3        "userIdentity": {
4            "type": "IAMUser",
5            "principalId": "AIDAMVNPBQA3EXAMPLE",
6            "arn": "arn:aws:iam::111111111111:user/bob",
7            "accountId": "111111111111",
8            "accessKeyId": "AKIAIOSFODNN7EXAMPLE",
9            "userName": "bob"
10       },
11       "eventTime": "2017-01-18T21:42:44Z",
12       "eventSource": "organizations.amazonaws.com",
13       "eventName": "AttachPolicy",
14       "awsRegion": "us-east-1",
15       "sourceIPAddress": "192.168.0.1",
16       "userAgent": "Mozilla/5.0 (Macintosh; Intel Mac OS X 10_11_6) AppleWebKit/537.36 (KHTML,
             like Gecko) Chrome/55.0.2883.95 Safari/537.36",
17       "errorCode": "PolicyTypeNotEnabledException",
18       "errorMessage": "The given policy type ServiceControlPolicy is not enabled on the current
             view",
19       "requestParameters": {
20           "policyId": "p-examplepolicyid111",
21           "targetId": "ou-examplerootid111-exampleouid111"
22       },
23       "responseElements": null,
24       "requestID": "EXAMPLE8-90ab-cdef-fedc-ba987EXAMPLE",
25       "eventID": "EXAMPLE8-90ab-cdef-fedc-ba987EXAMPLE",
26       "eventType": "AwsApiCall",
27       "recipientAccountId": "111111111111"
28 }
```

Amazon CloudWatch Events

AWS Organizations can work with CloudWatch Events to raise "events" when administrator-specified actions occur in an organization. For example, because of the sensitivity of such actions, most administrators would want to be warned every time someone creates a new account in the organization, or when an administrator of a member account attempts to leave the organization. You can configure CloudWatch Events rules that look for these actions and then send the generated events to administrator-defined targets. Targets can be an Amazon SNS topic that emails or text messages its subscribers. You could also create an AWS Lambda function that logs the details of the action for your later review.

For a tutorial that shows how to enable CloudWatch Events to monitor key activity in your organization, see Tutorial: Monitor Important Changes to Your Organization with CloudWatch Events .

To learn more about CloudWatch Events, inclucing how to configure and enable it, see the Amazon CloudWatch Events User Guide.

AWS Organizations Reference

Use the topics in this section to find detailed reference information for various aspects of AWS Organizations.

Topics

- Limits of AWS Organizations
- AWS Managed Policies Available for Use with AWS Organizations
- Service Control Policy Syntax

Limits of AWS Organizations

This section specifies limits that affect AWS Organizations.

Limits on Names

The following are restrictions on names that you create in AWS Organizations, including names of accounts, organizational units (OUs), roots, and policies:

- They must be composed of Unicode characters
- They must not exceed 250 characters in length

Maximum and Minimum Values

The following are the default maximums for entities in AWS Organizations:

Number of AWS accounts in an organization	Varies. *If you need to increase your limit, you can contact AWS Support. In the upper-right corner of the console, choose Support, Support Center, and then choose Create case.* An invitation sent to an account counts against this limit. The count is returned if the invited account declines, the master account cancels the invitation, or the invitation expires.
Number of roots in an organization	1
Number of OUs in an organization	1,000
Number of policies in an organization	1,000
Maximum size of a service control policy (SCP) document	5,120 bytes. This includes all characters, including white space. You can remove all white space characters (such as spaces and line breaks) that are outside quotation marks to reduce the size of your SCP if you approach the limit.
OU maximum nesting in a root	5 levels of OUs deep under a root
Invitations sent in a 24 hour period	20
Number of member accounts you can create concurrently	5 — As soon as one finishes, you can start another, but only five can be in progress at a time.
Number of entities to which you can attach a policy	Unlimited

Expiration times for handshakes

The following are the timeouts for handshakes in AWS Organizations:

Invitation to join an organization	15 days
Request to enable all features in an organization	90 days

Handshake is deleted and no longer appears in lists	30 days after the handshake is completed

Number of policies that can be attached to an entity

The maximum depends on the policy type as well as the entity that you're attaching the policy to. The following table shows each policy type and the number of entities to which each can be attached:

Policy type	Policies per root	Policies per OU	Policies per account
Service control policy	5	5	5

Note

Currently, you can have only one root in an organization.

The minimum depends on the policy type. The following table shows each policy type and the minimum number of entities to which each can be attached:

Policy type	Minimum allowed attached to an entity
Service control policy	1 — Every entity must have at least one SCP attached at all times. You can't remove the last SCP from an entity.

AWS Managed Policies Available for Use with AWS Organizations

This section identifies the AWS-managed policies provided for your use to manage your administration. You can't modify or delete an AWS managed policy, but you can attach or detach them to entities in your organization as needed.

AWS Organizations Managed Service Control Policies

Service control policies (SCPs) are similar to IAM permission policies, but are a feature of AWS Organizations rather than IAM. You use SCPs in an organization as filters to limit what services and actions the users and roles in attached accounts can perform. You can attach SCPs to roots, organizational units (OUs), or accounts in your organization. You can create your own, or you can use the policies that IAM defines. You can see the list of policies in your organization on the Policies page on the Organizations console.

Important
Every root, OU, and account must have at least one SCP attached at all times.

Policy Name	Description	ARN
FullAWSAccess	Provides AWS Organizations master account access to member accounts.	arn:aws:iam::aws:policy/AWSFullAccess

Service Control Policy Syntax

Service control policies (SCPs) use a similar syntax to that used by IAM permission policies and resource-based policies (like Amazon S3 bucket policies). For more information about IAM policies and their syntax, see Overview of IAM Policies in the *IAM User Guide*.

An SCP is a plaintext file that is structured according to the rules of JSON. It uses the elements that are described in this section.

Note
All characters that you type count against the size limit of your SCP. The examples in this guide show the SCPs formatted with extra white space to improve their readability. However, to save space if your policy size approaches the limit, you can delete any white space, such as space characters and line breaks that are outside quotation marks.

For general information about how SCPs work, see About Service Control Policies.

Version Element

Every SCP must include a `Version` element with the value "2012-10-17". This is the same version value as the most recent version of IAM permission policies:

```
1    "Version": "2012-10-17",
```

Statement Element

An SCP consists of one or more `Statement` elements. You can have only one `Statement` keyword in a policy, but the value can be a JSON array of statements (surrounded by [ ] characters).

The following example shows a single statement that consists of single `Effect`, `Action`, and `Resource` elements:

```
1    "Statement": {
2        "Effect": "Allow",
3        "Action": "*",
4        "Resource": "*"
5    }
```

The following example includes two statements as an array list inside one `Statement` element. The first statement allows all actions, while the second denies any EC2 actions. The end result is that an administrator in the account can delegate any permission *except* those from EC2:

```
1    "Statement": [
2        {
3            "Effect": "Allow",
4            "Action": "*",
5            "Resource": "*"
6        },
7        {
8            "Effect": "Deny",
9            "Action": "ec2:*",
10           "Resource": "*"
11       }
12   ]
```

Effect Element

Each statement must contain one `Effect` element. The value can be either `Allow` or `Deny`. It affects any actions listed in the same statement.

The following example shows an SCP with a statement that contains an `Effect` with a value of `Allow` that permits account users to perform actions for the Amazon S3 service. This example is useful in an organization where the default `FullAWSAccess` policies are all detached so that permissions are implicitly denied by default. The end result is that it whitelists the Amazon S3 permissions for any attached accounts:

```
1  {
2      "Version": "2012-10-17",
3      "Statement": {
4          "Effect": "Allow",
5          "Action": "s3:*"
6      }
7  }
```

Note that even though it uses the same `Allow` value keyword as an IAM permission policy, in an SCP it doesn't actually grant a user permissions to do anything. Remember that an SCP is a filter that restricts what permissions can be used in an attached account. In the preceding example, even if a user in the account had the `AdministratorAccess` managed policy attached, the SCP limits *all* users in the account to only Amazon S3 actions.

Action Element

Each statement must contain one `Action` element. The value is a list (a JSON array) of strings that identify AWS services and actions that are allowed or denied by the statement.

Each string consists of the abbreviation for the service (such as "s3", "ec2", "iam", or "organizations"), in all lowercase, followed by a colon and then an action from that service. The actions are case-sensitive, and must be typed as shown in each service's documentation. Generally, they are all typed with each word starting with an uppercase letter and the rest lowercase. For example: `"s3:ListAllMyBuckets"`.

You also can use an asterisk as a wildcard to match multiple actions that share part of a name. The value `"s3:*"` means all actions in the Amazon S3 service. The value `"ec2:Describe*"` matches only the EC2 actions that begin with "Describe".

Note

In an SCP, the wildcard (*) character in an `Action` element can be used only by itself or at the end of the string. It can't appear at the beginning or middle of the string. Therefore, `"servicename:action*"` is valid, but `"servicename:*action"` and `"servicename:some*action"` are both invalid in SCPs.

The examples in the preceding sections show simple `Action` elements that use wildcards to enable an entire service. The following example shows an SCP with a statement that permits account administrators to delegate describe, start, stop, and terminate permissions for EC2 instances in the account. This is another example of a whitelist, and is useful when the default `Allow *` policies are *not* attached so that, by default, permissions are implicitly denied. If the default `Allow *` policy is still attached to the root, OU, or account to which the following policy is attached, the policy has no effect:

```
1  {
2      "Version": "2012-10-17",
3      "Statement": {
4          "Effect": "Allow",
5          "Action": [
6              "ec2:DescribeInstances", "ec2:DescribeImages", "ec2:DescribeKeyPairs",
7              "ec2:DescribeSecurityGroups", "ec2:DescribeAvailabilityZones", "ec2:RunInstances",
```

```
8          "ec2:TerminateInstances", "ec2:StopInstances", "ec2:StartInstances"
9       ],
10      "Resource": "*"
11  }
12 }
```

The following example shows how you can blacklist services that you don't want used in attached accounts. It assumes that the default `"Allow *"` SCPs are still attached to all OUs and the root. This example policy prevents the account administrators in attached accounts from delegating any permissions for the IAM, Amazon EC2, and Amazon RDS services. Any action from other services can be delegated as long as there isn't another attached policy that denies them:

```
1 {
2     "Version": "2012-10-17",
3     "Statement": {
4         "Effect": "Deny",
5         "Action": [ "iam:*", "ec2:*", "rds:*" ],
6         "Resource": "*"
7     }
8 }
```

Important

SCPs do *not* support the `NotAction` element available for IAM permission policies.

For a list of all the services and the actions that they support in both AWS Organizations SCPs and IAM permission policies, see AWS Service Actions and Condition Context Keys for Use in IAM Policies in the *IAM User Guide*.

Resource Element

You can specify only "*" in the `Resource` element of an SCP. You can't specify individual resource Amazon Resource Names (ARNs).

Principal Element

You cannot specify a `Principal` element in an SCP.

Condition Element

You cannot specify a `Condition` element in an SCP.

Troubleshooting AWS Organizations

If you encounter issues when working with AWS Organizations, consult the topics in this section.

Topics

- Troubleshooting General Issues
- Troubleshooting AWS Organizations Policies

Troubleshooting General Issues

Use the information here to help you diagnose and fix access-denied or other common issues that you might encounter when working with AWS Organizations.

Topics

- I get an "access denied" message when I make a request to AWS Organizations
- I get an "access denied" message when I make a request with temporary security credentials
- I get an "access denied" message when I try to leave an organization as a member account or remove a member account as the master account
- I get a "limit exceeded" message when I try to add an account to my organization
- I get an "organization is still initializing" message when I try to add an account to my organization
- Changes that I make aren't always immediately visible

I get an "access denied" message when I make a request to AWS Organizations

- Verify that you have permissions to call the action and resource that you have requested. An administrator must grant permissions by attaching an IAM policy to your IAM user or to a group that you're a member of. If the policy statements that grant those permissions include any conditions, such as time-of-day or IP address restrictions, you also must meet those requirements when you send the request. For information about viewing or modifying policies for an IAM user, group, or role, see Working with Policies in the *IAM User Guide*.
- If you are signing API requests manually (without using the AWS SDKs), verify that you have correctly signed the request.

I get an "access denied" message when I make a request with temporary security credentials

- Verify that the IAM user or role that you are using to make the request has the correct permissions. Permissions for temporary security credentials are derived from an IAM user or role, so the permissions are limited to those granted to the IAM user or role. For more information about how permissions for temporary security credentials are determined, see Controlling Permissions for Temporary Security Credentials in the *IAM User Guide*.
- Verify that your requests are being signed correctly and that the request is well formed. For details, see the toolkit documentation for your chosen SDK or Using Temporary Security Credentials to Request Access to AWS Resources in the *IAM User Guide*.
- Verify that your temporary security credentials haven't expired. For more information, see Requesting Temporary Security Credentials in the *IAM User Guide*.

I get an "access denied" message when I try to leave an organization as a member account or remove a member account as the master account

- You can remove a member account only after you enable IAM user access to billing in the member account. For more information, see Activating Access to the Billing and Cost Management Console in the *AWS Billing and Cost Management User Guide*.
- You can remove an account from your organization only if the account has the information required for it to operate as a standalone account. When you create an account in an organization using the AWS Organizations console, API, or AWS CLI commands, that information isn't automatically collected. For an account that you want to make standalone, you must accept the AWS Customer Agreement, choose a support plan, provide and verify the required contact information, and provide a current payment method. AWS uses the payment method to charge for any billable (not AWS Free tTier) AWS activity that occurs

while the account isn't attached to an organization. For more information, see Leaving an Organization as a Member Account.

I get a "limit exceeded" message when I try to add an account to my organization

There is a limit to the number of accounts that you can have in an organization. Deleted or closed accounts continue to count against this limit.

An invitation to join counts against the limit of accounts in your organization. The count is returned if the invited account declines, the master account cancels the invitation, or the invitation expires.

- Before you close or delete an AWS account, remove it from your organization so that it doesn't continue to count against your limit.
- Contact AWS Support to request a limit increase.

I get an "organization is still initializing" message when I try to add an account to my organization

If you receive this error and it's been over an hour since you created the organization, contact AWS Support.

Changes that I make aren't always immediately visible

As a service that is accessed through computers in data centers around the world, AWS Organizations uses a distributed computing model called eventual consistency. Any change that you make in AWS Organizations takes time to become visible from all possible endpoints. Some of the delay results from the time it takes to send the data from server to server or from replication zone to replication zone. AWS Organizations also uses caching to improve performance, but in some cases this can add time. The change might not be visible until the previously cached data times out.

Design your global applications to account for these potential delays and ensure that they work as expected, even when a change made in one location isn't instantly visible at another.

For more information about how some other AWS services are affected by this, consult the following resources:

- Managing Data Consistency in the *Amazon Redshift Database Developer Guide*
- Amazon S3 Data Consistency Model in the *Amazon Simple Storage Service Developer Guide*
- Ensuring Consistency When Using Amazon S3 and Amazon Elastic MapReduce for ETL Workflows in the AWS Big Data Blog
- EC2 Eventual Consistency in the *Amazon EC2 API Reference.*

Troubleshooting AWS Organizations Policies

Use the information here to help you diagnose and fix common errors found in AWS Organizations policies.

Service Control Policies

Service control policies (SCPs) in AWS Organizations are similar to IAM policies and share a common syntax. This syntax begins with the rules of JavaScript Object Notation (JSON). JSON describes an *object* with name and value pairs that make up the object. The IAM policy grammar builds on that by defining what names and values have meaning for, and are understood by, the AWS services that use policies to grant permissions.

AWS Organizations uses a subset of the IAM syntax and grammar. For details, see Service Control Policy Syntax.

Topics

- More than one policy object
- More than one Statement element

More than one policy object

An SCP must consist of one and only one JSON object. You denote an object by placing { } braces around it. Although you can nest other objects within a JSON object by embedding additional { } braces within the outer pair, a policy can contain only one outermost pair of { } braces. The following example is ***incorrect*** because it contains two objects at the top level (called out in *red*):

```
1  {
2    "Version": "2012-10-17",
3    "Statement":
4    {
5      "Effect":"Allow",
6      "Action":"ec2:Describe*",
7      "Resource":"*"
8    }
9  }
10 {
11   "Statement": {
12     "Effect": "Deny",
13     "Action": "s3:*",
14     "Resource": "*"
15   }
16 }
```

You can, however, meet the intention of the preceding example with the use of correct policy grammar. Instead of including two complete policy objects, each with its own `Statement` element, you can combine the two blocks into a single `Statement` element. The `Statement` element has an array of two objects as its value, as shown in the following example:

```
1  {
2    "Version": "2012-10-17",
3    "Statement": [
4      {
5        "Effect": "Allow",
6        "Action": "ec2:Describe*",
7        "Resource":" *"
```

```
 8      },
 9      {
10        "Effect": "Deny",
11        "Action": "s3:*",
12        "Resource": "*"
13      }
14    ]
15 }
```

This example cannot be further compressed into a `Statement` with one element because the two elements have different effects. Generally, you can combine statements only when the `Effect` and `Resource` elements in each statement are identical.

More than one Statement element

This error might at first appear to be a variation on the error in the preceding section. However, syntactically it's a different type of error. In the following example, there is only one policy object as denoted by a single pair of { } braces at the top level. However, that object contains two `Statement` elements within it.

An SCP must contain only one `Statement` element, consisting of the name (`Statement`) appearing to the left of a colon, followed by its value on the right. The value of a `Statement` element must be an object, denoted by { } braces, containing one `Effect` element, one `Action` element, and one `Resource` element. The following example is *incorrect* because it contains two `Statement` elements in the policy object:

```
 1 {
 2    "Version": "2012-10-17",
 3    "Statement": {
 4      "Effect": "Allow",
 5      "Action": "ec2:Describe*",
 6      "Resource": "*"
 7    },
 8    "Statement": {
 9      "Effect": "Deny",
10      "Action": "s3:*",
11      "Resource": "*"
12    }
13 }
```

Because a value object can be an array of multiple value objects, you can solve this problem by combining the two `Statement` elements into one element with an object array, as shown in the following example:

```
 1 {
 2    "Version": "2012-10-17",
 3    "Statement": [
 4      {
 5        "Effect": "Allow",
 6        "Action": "ec2:Describe*",
 7        "Resource":"*"
 8      },
 9      {
10        "Effect": "Deny",
11        "Action": "s3:*",
12        "Resource": "*"
13      }
14    ]
15 }
```

The value of the `Statement` element is an object array. The array in the example consists of two objects, each of which is a correct value for a `Statement` element. Each object in the array is separated by commas.

Calling the API by Making HTTP Query Requests

This section contains general information about using the Query API for AWS Organizations. For details about the API operations and errors, see the AWS Organizations API Reference.

Note

Instead of making direct calls to the AWS Organizations Query API, you can use one of the AWS SDKs. The AWS SDKs consist of libraries and sample code for various programming languages and platforms (Java, Ruby, .NET, iOS, Android, and more). The SDKs provide a convenient way to create programmatic access to AWS Organizations and AWS. For example, the SDKs take care of tasks such as cryptographically signing requests, managing errors, and retrying requests automatically. For information about the AWS SDKs, including how to download and install them, see Tools for Amazon Web Services.

The Query API for AWS Organizations lets you call service actions. Query API requests are HTTPS requests that must contain an `Action` parameter to indicate the operation to be performed. AWS Organizations supports GET and POST requests for all operations. That is, the API doesn't require you to use GET for some actions and POST for others. However, GET requests are subject to the limitation size of a URL. Although this limit is browser dependent, a typical limit is 2048 bytes. Therefore, for Query API requests that require larger sizes, you must use a POST request.

The response is an XML document. For details about the response, see the individual action pages in the AWS Organizations API Reference.

Topics

- Endpoints
- HTTPS Required
- Signing AWS Organizations API Requests

Endpoints

AWS Organizations has a single global API endpoint that is hosted in the US East (N. Virginia) Region: https://organizations.us-east-1.amazonaws.com

For more information about AWS endpoints and regions for all services, see Regions and Endpoints in the *AWS General Reference*.

HTTPS Required

Because the Query API returns sensitive information such as security credentials, you must use HTTPS to encrypt all API requests.

Signing AWS Organizations API Requests

Requests must be signed using an access key ID and a secret access key. We strongly recommend that you don't use your AWS root account credentials for everyday work with AWS Organizations. You can use the credentials for an IAM user or temporary credentials such as you use with an IAM role.

To sign your API requests, you must use AWS Signature Version 4. For information about using Signature Version 4, see Signature Version 4 Signing Process in the *AWS General Reference*.

AWS Organizations doesn't support earlier versions, such as Signature Version 2.

For more information, see the following:

- AWS Security Credentials – Provides general information about the types of credentials that you can use to access AWS
- IAM Best Practices – Offers suggestions for using the IAM service to help secure your AWS resources, including those in AWS Organizations
- Temporary Credentials – Describes how to create and use temporary security credentials

Document History for AWS Organizations

The following table describes major documentation updates for AWS Organizations.

- **API version: 2016-11-28**

Change	Description	Date
New services for trusted access	AWS Config and AWS Firewall Manager added as services that can work with the accounts in your organization.	April 18, 2018
Trusted service access	You can now enable or disable access for select AWS services to work in the accounts in your organization. AWS SSO is the initial supported trusted service.	March 29, 2018
Account removal is now self-service	You can now remove accounts that were created from within AWS Organizations without contacting AWS Support.	December 19, 2017
Added support for new service AWS Single Sign-On	AWS Organizations now supports integration with AWS Single Sign-On (AWS SSO).	December 7, 2017
AWS added a service-linked role to all organization accounts	A service-linked role named `AWSServiceRoleForOrganizat` is added to all accounts in an organization to enable integration between AWS Organizations and other AWS services.	October 11, 2017
You can now remove created accounts	Customers can now remove created accounts from their organization, with help from AWS Support.	June 15, 2017
Service Launch	Initial version of the AWS Organizations documentation that accompanied the launch of the new service.	February 17, 2017

AWS Glossary

For the latest AWS terminology, see the AWS Glossary in the *AWS General Reference*.